Reaching
Generation Next

Other books by Lewis A. Drummond

Leading Your Church in Evangelism
Eight Keys to Biblical Revival
The Awakening That Must Come
Spurgeon: Prince of Preachers
Ripe for Harvest
The Evangelist
Women of Awakenings
The Spiritual Woman
The Canvas Cathedral

Reaching
Generation Next

Effective Evangelism in Today's Culture

Lewis A. Drummond

 Baker Books

A Division of Baker Book House Co
Grand Rapids, Michigan 49516

Published by Baker Books
a division of Baker Book House Company
P.O. Box 6287, Grand Rapids, MI 49516-6287

Printed in the United States of America

Library of Congress Cataloging-in-Publication Data

Drummond, Lewis A.
    Reaching generation next : effective evangelism in today's culture / Lewis
A. Drummond.
       p.   cm.
    Includes bibliographical references.
    ISBN 0-8010-9151-9 (pbk.)
    1. Evangelistic work. 2. Postmodernism—Religious aspects—Christianity.
I. Title.
    BV3793 .D78 2002
    269′ .2—dc21
                                      2002009994

A word to our postmodern day:

I observe that you are very religious. . . . I . . . found an altar with this inscription, "TO AN UNKNOWN GOD." Therefore what you worship in ignorance, this I proclaim to you.

Acts 17:22–23

Contents

Foreword

As the new millennium gets under way, evangelical Christians find themselves categorical thinkers in a noncategorical age. Taking the gospel to a world whose citizens see themselves as "special cases" of individuality where no universal codes apply is going to require the most sensitive and creative approaches to evangelism.

Lewis Drummond has been involved in both personal and mass evangelism for the past several decades. During those years he has observed the continual changes of the sociological fabric of Western culture. We have moved from the high years of cultural pride in the fifties, through the dyspepsia of the Vietnam years, to the blasé cultural indifference of the nineties, and finally to the return of patriotism in 2001. In every age his has been an important voice on how to reach out to a culture in hasty transition.

But the arrival of the postmodern mind-set has presented a particularly difficult challenge. Postmoderns have accepted their category while denying they can be categorized. They reject all one-size-fits-all theology. As they see themselves, each of them is too much an individual to admit to any one-for-all approach. Hell and heaven—and how one gets to one and avoids the other—they say cannot be cut from a single notion of how one comes to Christ. They feel there are no "spiritual laws" that apply to all people.

Further, postmoderns have a "code of individual sovereignty." That is, they generally feel that people are all right pretty much as they are. Who has the right to require anyone else to believe what they believe— even about eternity—or how we get converted? Evangelism among many postmoderns is seen to be evil, because they assume that people are okay just as they are, and to try to make them what we think they ought to be is presumptuous and arrogant, even for the nobler causes of Christianity.

Postmoderns are multicultural, and they prize ethnic and religious identity. Christ may be noble and worthy of esteem, they say, but he is not above Buddha or Mohammed. Most postmoderns would also say, "Christians must stop trying to change the world with the kinds of aggressive evangelistic techniques that they used in the old nineteenth century. They must accede that no two possible converts can be handled in the same way or be forced to face one universal set of conversion requirements.

Lewis Drummond has done a good job with diagnosis and prescription in this study. This book may be a pacesetter on the subject of how we are to approach an age stuck in the gospel-avoidance mode. This book will help you understand how postmodern evangelization is to be done. But, as Dr. Drummond suggests, to follow God in fulfilling Christ's command to the church will require more than a mere reading of any book. It will require a sensitive obedience to the Holy Spirit of God.

Calvin Miller

Preface

There is perhaps no theme that has captured the interest and imagination of the contemporary church quite as profoundly as the concept of evangelism. Nor is any theme more at the core of Christianity than evangelism. It consumed our Lord. That is why he came. It should, therefore, grip us at the very heart of our faith. Thankfully, that which was once ignored or even ridiculed by some has now become the concern of most enlightened Christians. God's people are coming alive to the fact that the church evangelizes or it dies. It is that serious. And although it may be true that some of the motives that have spurred this new impetus are not as high or spiritual as one would wish, nonetheless, evangelism has become of vital interest to most Christians today, and for that we must thank our Lord. After all, he is the one who inspires the endeavor.

The purpose of this volume is to place in the hands of the Christian leader—and the average layperson—a basic work on the essential aspects of the evangelistic enterprise and to provide foundational guidelines on how to evangelize in a local church in today's new world. We do live in a new day. It has been called, among other things, postmodernism or the Generation X era. The people of this generation, as well as the next generation that is rapidly growing up, must be reached.

This book has a practical as well as a theological purpose. The primary theme of the work is that the whole church stands at the fountainhead of the evangelistic tide in God's kingdom. The church holds the key to successful outreach. Therefore, each believer must become an "evangelist" in a deep and profound sense. Elucidating this essential truth, the book attempts to guide God's people and his church into a dynamic evangelistic program to reach the new age.

Moreover, there has arisen a fresh openness to spiritual things. Perhaps the terrorism and other calamities of our day, such as the September 11, 2001, attack in America, have cracked open a new door for the gospel. Regardless of what is occurring, this new generation is asking questions. And the church has the answer. It is Jesus Christ.

I must not close this brief preface without expressing my gratitude to the faithful secretaries at Beeson Divinity School. To them I acknowledge my debt. Above all, I express my gratitude to Janice Jordan who labored over the computer for hours getting the manuscript in place. Her work was invaluable. To Paul Baxter I express gratitude for permitting me to draw material from the book we coauthored, *Responding to the Skeptic*. I also thank my colleague and friend Calvin Miller for the foreword.

So I present my concept of the church's evangelistic task for today with the prayer that God will use it to inspire and help us all to "do the work of an evangelist" (2 Tim. 4:5).

one

Today's Emerging World

Over thirty years ago I had the privilege of publishing my first book on evangelism. Those days witnessed the beginning of a revolutionary time. Western culture found itself in disturbing flux. In America the Boomers were on the scene with their deep reaction to Vietnam and the old traditions. The Iron Curtain held sway in Eastern Europe and seemed far from coming down, even though cracks and erosion began to appear. Modernity still reigned, but new ideas quickly began filling the cracks that were forming in the worldview of the moderns, a worldview that had held sway since the birth of the Renaissance. Yet, as is often the case, it seemed that many churches were almost oblivious to the ferment bubbling up all around them. They, who could have made a compelling contribution to the turbulent hour, often failed to rise to the challenge.

In that first volume I related the story that came out of the American Revolution of the eighteenth century. The tale seemed an apt illustration of the scene at that time. Washington Irving wrote a parody that unfolds in a fascinating fashion. Old Rip Van Winkle, from a small New England town, trekked one day up into the Catskill Mountains. Exhausted by the hike, he sat down on a grassy knoll and fell fast asleep. He dreamed on and on. When he finally awoke, he realized it was late and he must hurry home. As he walked into his village, strange sights greeted his eyes. Nothing seemed the same; he puzzled over what could have happened. The streets were changed, he recognized few houses, and everything appeared so different. Slowly it dawned on the old slumberer that he had actually been asleep twenty years. During those long years, the American colonies had revolted against British rule and won their freedom. He was now living in the radically new United States of America. Poor old Rip had slept through the Revolution.

Irving's imaginary tale seemed quite apt in the days of the sixties and seventies of century twenty. But the story is even more applicable today in century twenty-one. The fact that the contemporary church finds itself living and attempting to minister in a revolutionary atmosphere should be obvious to all. It is a different day than several decades ago. So-called postmodernism is taking over, and the church once again finds itself in the grip of a social and cultural revolution of gigantic proportions. So I have put my hand to a complete rewriting of my first volume, which has become this work. I do so because everything seems to be in a state of radical change. All aspects of society are once again in flux. Foundations of modernism, long accepted as valid even in the earlier Boomer years of the 1950s, are being seriously shaken. No segment of societal traditions escapes scrutiny and questioning. The more traditional, older generation is still with us, yet discerning minds agree that nothing will ever be quite the same again. Western society is rapidly changing, but the most disquieting element of the sociological, philosophical, and cultural revolution centers in the fact that often the sleeping Rip Van Winkle of the hour is none other than many contemporary churches. God's people, who should be on the cutting edge of the radically changing scene and moving our new age toward God, are often found slumbering away on some grassy knoll of irrelevance, or even denial, while the world all but fragments around them.

In the light of such a situation, the church must be awakened to the contemporary cultural atmosphere so that it can address itself to the problems this social and philosophical revolution precipitates. Although much has been written on postmodernism for the individual reader to absorb, in the final analysis, the church as a whole must get geared for the new challenge it faces, hence the writing of this book on the subject.

This does not mean that every church has its head in the sand and is thus oblivious to the dramatic scenario. Often the church just finds itself in the grip of irrelevancy, failing to address and communicate effectively

to today's worldview. If such is the case, the church must be awakened
and updated. The people of God must be shaken from their slumbers
and made to see and respond to the tremendous evangelistic challenge
of this turbulent hour. It may be that the disturbing voices being heard
in our world today will be the ones to awaken the sleepers. There is openness, as we shall see, to spiritual matters in this hour that bodes well for
a dynamic evangelism of integrity. Perhaps these voices will give the
people of God the urgent wake-up call needed.

A New Day

The revolution of our era, a worldview that is now well under way,
has acquired its own moniker; we commonly call it *postmodernism*. As
many realize, in the late 1960s the modern era pretty well died and postmodernism commenced its reign. Its constituents, generally speaking,
are those born after 1965, often called Generation X or Busters, and the
next generation, the children of the Busters, are following in their foot-
steps. They are all a different sort with a different approach to life and
reality than that of older generations. Sociologists and others tell us that
this new spirit has come about as a reaction to the sterility of modernism,
or so-called modernity, the socialized, philosophical, rational mind-set
that grew out of the Enlightenment movement. This understanding of
life and value postmodernity has rejected. And the reaction is basic and
fundamental, ushering in an entirely new worldview. Since one's worldview determines life values and meaning, the challenge for the evangelical church today is to confront the validity of the new worldview.
Can the church convince postmoderns that Christianity offers the best
of all worldviews? The future growth and effectiveness of the church
depend largely on how it responds to that challenge, not to mention the
spiritual condition of an entire generation that must be reached for
Christ.

So the question becomes, What are these postmoderns and their
young children saying? We clearly need to understand them before we
can effectively communicate Christ's message to them. We shall delve
into that issue, attempting to acquire at least an overview of the movement from a basic philosophical perspective. It may appear somewhat
pedantic to review these philosophical issues, but all people, regardless
of their sophistication, have a philosophy that determines their worldview. Philosophy is important, so we will take a short excursion into the
basic thought patterns of postmodernism. But before launching out on

that voyage, it will be helpful to see what the postmoderns are in revolt against, namely, *modernity.*

The Meaning of Modernity

Space precludes a thorough philosophical—or practical—investigation of modernity; that would require countless volumes, and much has been written on the subject. But the essence of modernity, its essential worldview, advocates the epistemological principle that truth and reality can be discerned primarily by the five senses and through rationalism. Empiricism (sense perception) and rationalism stand as the central sources and final criteria of truth. This philosophy had its contemporary birth, as stated, in the spirit of the Renaissance and the Enlightenment.

It must be understood that epistemology, how truth is discerned, always constitutes the essential question in the quest for a meaningful life. Many philosophers of the relatively recent past and a fair number of contemporary ones have enrolled in the Enlightenment school of thought. Tragically, they often reject spiritual realities. These thinkers tend to take this rigid line because metaphysical, spiritual concepts raise questions, the answers to which are not totally verifiable on a mere rational or empirical level. Thus they either outright reject spiritual truths or at least minimize them. Many see them as merely irrelevant.

The philosophical departments in European and American universities have been more or less committed to some form of rational-empirical thought for years, at least until quite recent times. The result is that philosophy has suffered in proportion to the many vital issues it has ignored. Moreover, it seems abundantly clear that, during the pervasive reign of modernity, many average people, especially of the older generations, have shared the same attitude toward rational-empirical thought, even if with an unsophisticated understanding. Thus we have our American obsession with the scientific, materialistic, affluent society—the "good life."

This epistemological approach to truth and reality has interesting early roots. Aspects can be seen in certain Greek thinkers like Aristotle with his logical dialectical method. It should be realized that confidence in human knowledge goes back to very early thought. As New Testament scholar C. H. Dodd points out, "In the classical period an almost unbounded confidence in the human reason led thinkers to believe that accurate knowledge of reality was attainable and that in such knowledge lay the ideal for human life."[1] This sounds very much like the modernity that emerged in and out of the Enlightenment. However, it became clear to some Greek thinkers that such an approach did not answer some very important questions of life. Consequently there arose in some circles a philosophical turn to *revelation*—the "knowledge of God." Thus emerged *gnosticism*, but that approach never led to a *true* knowledge of God. As Dodd goes on to state, they believe that "eternal life lies in the knowledge of God, but they overlook the explicit teaching of the Gospel about the true nature of such knowledge."[2]

In more recent years, modernism was more or less epitomized in the utterly radical rationalism of Friedrich Hegel. This philosopher, whose dictum declared "the rational is real and the real is rational," has influenced Western thinking tremendously. His approach reached its peak in the logical positivism of scholars like A. J. Ayer, Bertrand Russell, and others with their "verifiable principle." They held that any proposition that is claimed to be true must be verifiable by rational or empirical methodologies; otherwise it is meaningless. So influential did this extreme approach become that both the professional philosopher and many common people alike all but worship before the shrine of this scientific, rational approach to truth, reality, and meaning.

Now no one wishes to decry the amazing advance and benefit that scientific, empirical investigation has produced. We enjoy, and rightly so, the good things of the affluent society. But modernity has built its entire system of values on this level, and this is where the problems arise for the postmoderns and the church as well. By ignoring or minimizing the reality of spiritual values, or by classifying them as meaningless, modernity has defined reality on a quite materialistic basis. Health and wholeness are often sought primarily through scientific medicine and behavioristic psychology. Status, and therefore acceptance by one's peers, means the attainment of certain economic levels. In the spirit of the philosopher Hegel, these devotees of an empirical worldview believe that all problems, in principle if not yet in fact, can finally be solved in the laboratory or on the psychiatrist's couch. Though the average man on the street may not be able, as can the philosopher, to present a formal rationale for such a completely empirical, rational approach to truth and reality, he has certainly lived out such an approach on a practical level. Thus the modernist dreams of the entire world being well fed, in good health, living long, and enjoying all the benefits of life to the fullest and is not concerned with eternity.

Faced with this purely empirical and rationalistic-scientific worldview, the church's efforts in evangelism are hindered, unless God's people can find a convincing apologetic for the faith to combat the basic tenets of modernism. For example, the so-called conflict between science and religion that has caused many to cast their vote for behaviorism and the laboratory instead of for the pulpit still waits to be resolved. The effective evangelistic church must come up with a credible answer and apologetic for this approach, not to mention the crying need for an effective apologetic to address postmodernism. And too many churches have not faced or developed a convincing apologetic as to the essential presuppositions of what constitutes truth. Again, may it be said, the epistemological problem is the basic issue. Where can an answer be found? Is there a convincing apologetic to knock down the straw men standing in the way of an acceptance of the gospel of Jesus Christ for the modern's, not to mention the postmodern's, mind-set? Yes, as Francis Schaeffer has correctly pointed out:

> The floodwaters of secular thought . . . overwhelmed the church because the leaders did not understand the importance of combating a false set of presuppositions. They largely fought the battle on the wrong ground and so, instead of being far ahead in both defense and communication, they lagged woefully behind. . . . Man thinks differently concerning truth, and so now for us, more than ever before, a presuppositional apologetic is imperative.[3]

This opens up a whole new vista of thought. Of course, the place of apologetics in evangelism is a subject in and of itself. It will be approached later in this book in some depth, but that must be put on hold for the moment. What is essential to see at the immediate juncture centers in what modernity is and why postmoderns reject it. So, we carry on, looking now at another aspect of modernity.

Humanism

Another voice that sallies forth from the modern mind-set centers in humanism, i.e., the concept holding that life is to be understood in purely human terms. Naturally this emerges out of a rational, empirical epistemology. There have always been committed humanists, of course, but they usually tend to stay in their ivory towers or in relatively small, esoteric groups. Since the Enlightenment, however, this worldview has become quite widespread. Perhaps one of the reasons humanism as an orientation to life moved out of the philosopher's ivory tower and into the marketplace is because of the influence of behavioristic psychology and thought. The modernity movement, coupled with the industrial revolution in its depersonalization of people, caused the human character to cry out desperately for recognition. Behaviorism was born. What developed was a sort of romantic, materialistic view of human personality. Growing out of this basic approach, humanism declares that "the real," and thus anything of ultimate value, rests in the human person-ality and human interests. This has clearly been a modernist life view, especially since Freud.

Of course postmodernism has some roots here as well. It must be granted that an element of truth can be found in humanism, as it can in pure scientism. Everyone should find sympathy with philanthropic endeavors to enhance human dignity and meet the pressing needs of one's fellowman. People are important; they are important to God. But when materialistic, rationalistic humanism becomes a worldview that excludes God and spiritual values as the ultimate good and romanti-cizes "enlightened man," trouble begins for the evangel. But that is what a commitment to a rational-empirical humanistic epistemology will do, and that gets right to the heart of modernity.

Existentialism

Voices were raised against a crass rational-empirical humanistic worldview, even in the heyday of modernity. One voice that was heard—and still is heard because it possesses postmodernity overtones—can be called *agnostic existentialism*. The existentialist, in oversimplified terms, sees existence as more important than essence. Experience is where real-ity can be found. Drain from each moment of existence all the good it has to offer. Whatever turns you on or makes you happy matters most. Objective standards are out; inner truth is where life's meaning can be found. The autonomous self reigns.

This worldview has a certain kinship to humanism, but it has its own way of expressing itself and viewing life, and rather than leading to a kind of proud utopianism and optimism as did scientific empiricism, it tends to lead to serious, almost morbid despair. Agnostic existentialists hold that the chaos of this world presents a universe with no ultimate reality, order, or meaning. Objective realities and principles are laid aside or ignored. Failing to look beyond the immediacy of temporal exis-tence, deep despair can easily ensue. Still, the practical conclusion of this orientation to life is in essence the same as that of the hard-nosed empiricist or humanist, namely, no God. As Martin Heidegger has expressed it, we came from nothing and we go to nothing. Jean Paul Sartre said that nothing can save us from ourselves. Friedrich Nietzsche claimed God was dead.

Thus one is constantly thrown back on one's self. The views espoused by philosophers such as Nietzsche and Heidegger and popularized in the mid-twentieth century by writers like Albert Camus and Sartre, impacted many and created a new and different worldview. It may be that not all who live in this general frame of reference are propositional atheists. Yet, because they believe that self, not God, reigns, they are something of at least a practical atheist or agnostic as far as everyday living is concerned.

At the same time, these thinkers have rejected philosophical rationalism, and in a modified sense even empiricism, as the ways to truth and meaning. It begins to look somewhat like postmodernism, although the postmoderns are more positive and less in despair than the extreme existentialists. Actually, existentialism has made its significant contribution to the postmodern spirit, as we shall see shortly. The crunch for the church, however, is that these existentialists reject the concept of *revealed truth*, which is clearly a central Christian position. So with little or nothing left to build on, except their own selves, they just opt out. This is their decision of "courage" in order to become an "authentic self." We meet many like that yet today in the traffic pattern of everyday life. Here is where we still find a host of people, especially the Boomers, whether they are of the revolutionary sixties or the strange, passive seventies. Little wonder we call them the "me generation." Granted, many of them have not worked out their position in thoughtful terms; still existentialism describes their basic approach to life. And if the church thinks them to be no more than immoral reactionaries who should thus be held up to scorn and contempt, it will miss evangelizing a segment of society that desperately needs the gospel.

All this does not mean that all existentialists are as radical as Heidegger and company. There is Christian existentialism, personified in men like Søren Kierkegaard. But that is another subject, and space again forbids it being addressed here. The point is that modernism in its various forms still remains with us, even if it is becoming passé to the postmodern mind.

All this raises the issue of what the fallout of the modernity movement has been, especially for the emerging generation. The only answer that can be given today is that there has been a reasonably strong reaction, namely, *postmodernity*. And therein lies the challenge for the church in its evangelism for the new millennium.

The Postmoderns

As previously pointed out, myriad books have been produced in recent years on the essence of the postmodern spirit. It seems hardly necessary, therefore, to go into minute detail in analyzing and describing the postmodern's worldview. Yet a general sweep of the basic thought of postmodernism stands in order for today's church. Hopefully it will not be too generalized and the heart of the issue can be set forth so that the church can launch out on its challenge to evangelize this growing segment of society.

D. A. Carson has given a succinct definition of postmodernism in his perceptive volume *The Gagging of God*. A rather lengthy quote from Carson's work will help us think in this direction and give us a working grasp of the postmodern worldview. And remember, one's worldview dictates one's understanding of truth, reality, and life. That is important. Carson wrote:

> The branches of this highly heterogeneous movement have certain features in common. Most visions of "god" in the movement are pantheistic; some are tied to ecology or to the more radical strains of feminism. The aim is not to be reconciled to a transcendent God, who has made us and against whom we have rebelled, but to grow in self-awareness and self-fulfillment, to become self-actualized, to grow to our full potential, until we are rather more at one with the god/universe than we otherwise would be. The focus, in short, is self; evil is reinterpreted and thus emasculated; and any notion of judgment imposed by a personal/transcendent God whose wrath has been and will be displayed, is utterly repugnant. Thus "spirituality," a popular notion that enjoys full scope even in the *New York Times Book Review*, is divorced from any biblically faithful worldview. Needless to say, there is no need for a mediator let alone a suffering priest who takes our sin on himself.
>
> There are at least two important implications for the preacher of the gospel. The first is that a person who is largely biblically illiterate but who has absorbed substantial doses of New Age theosophy will hear us to be saying things we do not really mean. If we talk about God, Spirit, new birth, power, abundant life, peace, joy, love, family life, conscience, faith, trust, and a host of other topics, they will all be nicely slotted into a New Age framework. Even words like "sin" will be read as "bad things" or perhaps "bad karma"—but not at all as something whose badness derives from its offensiveness to the God who has made us and to whom we must give an account. The entire structure of thought of such a person guarantees that he or she will hear us quite differently from what we intend to say, what we think we are saying. "Sin" is a snicker word—that is, it conveys nothing of odium, but makes people snicker. Millions of men and women fornicate without the slightest qualms of conscience.
>
> The second implication is that many ostensible believers inside our churches—some of whom are genuine believers and some of whom are not—have inevitably picked up some of the surrounding chatter and, being poorly grounded in Scripture and theology, have incorporated into their understanding of Christianity some frankly incompatible elements. Remarkably many notions of "spirituality" abound; very few ask, for

instance, what a "spiritual" life looks like *according to the New Testament documents*. In this framework there is going on . . . a battle for the mind, even though many have not perceived the nature of the fight.[4]

This is revolutionary. Remember, in the late 1960s the modern era essentially died, at least as far as the new generation is concerned. And when a society dies, that precipitates a revolution. But why did post-modernism arise on the ashes of modernity in the first place? The answer is simple, yet quite profound: Modernism does not produce everything it promises. There is more to truth and reality than empiricism and rationalism can describe. It gave us new technology, but it did not produce a better person. Materialism and humanism are not the final answers to the meaningful life.

Stanley Grenz, in his *A Primer on Postmodernism*, lays out the roots of the rise of the movement. He contends it has its essential theses in the so-called deconstructionism movement. Modernity's epistemological assumptions, as we have seen, assert that rationalism and empiricism give us all the knowledge we need to discover what is objectively true and good. And it can all be discovered by the human mind. Reason reigns in all areas of life; moreover, the knowledge attained by such methods is true and objective and good. It really is an optimistic worldview. That approach, as seen, found its clearest expression in the German thinker Friedrich Hegel. But after the attack of Nietzsche and others, serious questions arose; and postmodern *deconstruction* set in.

Although the deconstructionists began their work in the literary sphere, e.g., Sartre, Albert Camus, and Heidegger, it soon spread to all areas of thought. The modernists hold that all societies and cultures "possess a common, invariant structure."[5] This tenet the deconstructionists reject. They hold that any proposition is interpreted by the one who considers it. The interpreter gets in dialogue with the proposition, and thus it can have different meanings for different "interpreters." This is revolutionary, for as Grenz points out: "Postmodern philosophers applied these theories . . . to the world as a whole. . . . Reality will be read differently by each knowing self that encounters it. This means that there is no one meaning of the world, no transcendent center to reality as a whole.[6]

The implications of this epistemological assumption are tremendous. It means there are *no pure objectives or absolutes*. Truth is *relative* to the individual. Morals, ethics, and other propositions are relative to one's own opinion and interpretation. God and faith, therefore, are relative. *All* is relative, even objective "good." Evangelist Billy Graham bemoaned the fact back in 1973 in an Amsterdam evangelism conference that the young people have deserted any absolute truth. Even knowledge is not inherently good or objectively valid for all. Inevitable progress to the good life becomes a fanciful dream. The Enlightenment is out.

Some interpret the postmodern mentality as something of a return to premodern thinking. That may well be true—and in some respects good. Nonetheless, there are clearly many negatives. Increasingly, a sense of chaos as over against the stability of modernity has set in. Many postmoderns do not trust the traditional—institutions, jobs, the church, and the future. Postmodernism creates a rather pessimistic worldview, but not to the depth of the pure existentialists. There are those in the postmodern philosophy who say we can really know little if anything with absolute certainty, thus they tend to downplay or outrightly reject the gospel. However, as one writer in a philosophical periodical put it:

> The postmodern recognition of the limits of rationality (and the humility of spirit that recognition necessarily entails) need not lead us to conclude that there is no truth or that we are incapable of knowing truth. There is an important difference between, on the one hand, saying that there is a gap between our knowledge and true reality and, on the other hand, saying that such a gap is so profound that there is no sense in which our knowledge of reality can be said to be adequate. One sees through the glass darkly, though one still *sees*—it is not as if there is no sight at all. The sight is provisional and imperfect, meaning that it is always open to the possibility of reproof and correction. The resulting *adequatio* is—technically speaking—profoundly inadequate; yet it still remains practically adequate. Perhaps we should follow Gorgias here and speak of a "provisional *logo.*" Instead of seeing reason as something that we master and also use to master the world and God, we might better take reason to be something in which we *participate* but do not claim as our own.
>
> St. Thomas Aquinas (1224–1274) reminds us of an important tension here that must not be lost. On the one hand, Christians affirm the possibility of knowing about God and even knowing Him in a personal way. Since we are made in God's image, our intellects are capable of understanding God to some extent.[7]

Paradoxically, in the postmodern denial of absolutes, they have actually created a set of their own absolutes. Author William D. Watkins insightfully sees them as follows:

> Freedom from religion
> Death a beautiful choice
> I do—for now
> Family is who you come home to
> Love the one you're with
> I am a woman, hear me roar
> Race colors everything

History in the remaking
The politically correct life[8]

Watson is quite correct. These concepts, which form the postmoderns' worldview, are their substitute for true absolutes. We all must have absolutes whether we deny their existence or not. Everyone makes his or her own worldview, and absolutes are the ingredients thereof. What a tragedy when people build on the shifting sands of their own ego.

As a case in point, look at the moral issue.

The Moral Issue

Perhaps the most disturbing issue to the average Christian is the strange milieu in which contemporary ethics finds itself. This morass grows out of the postmodern spirit of *relativism*, the concept that there are no absolutes, such as objective moral principles. This basic presupposition has been adopted by most postmoderns. Even the traditional systems of logic have fallen to the ground. As we know, the first move in classical logical thought is: If you have A, it is not non-A. But as Schaeffer says, "If you understand the extent to which this no longer holds sway, you will understand our present situation."[9] There simply are no absolutes we are told, and this applies directly to moral principles. Ernest Hemingway expressed it like this: "What is moral is what you feel good after. What is evil is what you feel bad after."[10] Subjectivism makes the decision concerning appropriate action. It was in something of this atmosphere that situation ethics emerged with its rejection of absolute, ethical standards. So as young people are urged to do their thing, established principles of moral right and wrong are laid aside.

The committed postmodern will argue that there is no reason to believe that ethical standards came down from heaven, inscribed in stone, and are absolute for all people. The individual thus becomes the discerner of right and wrong. Every person can set his or her own standards. Value systems, like states and civilizations, come and go. They are conditioned by their history and have no claim to finality. It's true that some cultural concepts need to be questioned; however, because of the spirit of relativism in ethics that postmoderns espouse, many of the great biblical principles of moral right have been swept away in the avalanche. In the light of this disappearance of objective, securely grounded values, it is little wonder that Paul Tillich called this world a "land of broken symbols." The consequence of it all centers in the fact that today such confusion reigns in ethics that everyone seems to be in a state of moral turmoil, from the thinker in his isolated study to the young person in his or her own little self-oriented world. If ever an age was ethically and morally adrift on a sea of uncertainty, the postmodern age epitomizes it. The average postmodern declares: You can decide what works for you, what is good and bad for yourself. Moral confusion obviously results, and the best word to describe the post–1965 revolution is chaos. Gone are the quiet, orderly ways of the previous generations. The American dream fades.

This postmodern understanding of objective truth exerts its influence on multitudes. It presents real social and generational problems. Case in point: Older adults tend to hold in contempt young people who may advocate worthy social issues, because after the discussion the young people go to bed together. By the same token, young people display contempt for the older view of sexual morality because many of its advocates are seemingly blind to pressing social problems, which young people consider more important moral issues. Morality is judged on how one sees or interprets specific issues. The result is that young postmoderns cannot relate to their Boomer parents. The generation gap widens, family life erodes, and the problem only deepens.

Postmoderns cry out for meaningful relationships. If they do not get them at home, they turn elsewhere—some even to the computer. And tragically, as the gap grows wider, the church seems less and less able to evangelize effectively. It must awaken to what is going on.

If Socrates was right when he said, "The unexamined life is not worth living," many are living rather worthless lives, because when absolutes fly out the epistemological window, how can one find an objective criteria with which to judge or examine propositions? It seems fair to say that postmoderns, in the final analysis, are pure existential pragmatists. If a thing or thought "works" or pleases them, they uncritically accept it. The results are that the bulk of people live a simple, practical, secular life. Yet at the same time it must be granted, as Craig Miller argues:

> It is not as pessimistic or as negative as one might at first think. In many ways this view is more realistic than the scientific, rationalistic perspective of the modern era. It has a human dimension to it. It asks: How does progress affect people? It wonders who really benefits when a new invention is offered. It muses about whether it is time to step back from the future and to ask what this all means to us, today.
>
> The postmodern perspective is one that questions every tenet of the modern era. It is a view of the world that is adroit at asking questions, while not necessarily providing the answers.[11]

To question modernity is commendable. But with no objective absolutes, there is little wonder postmoderns have neither answers nor sound alternatives.

This basic understanding of truth and reality has profound spiritual implications. If each person selects his or her own criterion of meaning, one can accept or reject spiritual truths as he or she thinks wise—and this includes Christian truth. The reaction of the confirmed postmodern when faced with the biblical truth of Jesus Christ is, "That is good for you, but I see it differently." Some even have quite rebellious attitudes toward the Christian worldview. The result is that, because of their particular worldview (which means rejection of absolute truth), they simply turn away from the gospel, believing it is perfectly correct for them to do so if they wish. At the same time among many postmoderns, there is a new quest for spirituality, at least of some sort.

The Quest for Spirituality

Today, paradoxically, there seems to be a hunger, even a quest, for spiritual reality. For many the approach of modernity has not produced the "good life." That is what lies at the core of the postmodern's rejection of modernism. Rationalism, empiricism, existential humanism, and the entire approach of modernity have failed to provide a life of meaning. Thus they seek for some spiritual reality that will answer their pressing needs. Feeling adrift on a sea of uncertainty, they want their empty lives filled with something satisfying. But are they finding it? If not, why?

The postmodern worldview, as has been contended by some thinkers, is actually no worldview at all. Therein is the problem—of course, it is a worldview. Everyone has some sort of worldview, but the postmodern's view is a strange one to say the least, offering little but emptiness. The postmodern's quest for meaningful spiritual realities, however, may well give the church a great opportunity to share the ultimate truth of Christ that gives life to the fallen.

In the *Birmingham (Alabama) News,* October 29, 1999, a feature article by Greg Garrison was printed with this headline: "Birmingham Novelist Takes Readers on a New Spiritual Adventure . . ."

> With 10 million copies of *The Celestine Prophecy* in print and 6 million of its sequel, *The Tenth Insight,* spiritual novelist James Redfield has become an international celebrity.
>
> The soft-spoken Birmingham native, who maintains a home on a lake surrounded by pine trees near Saginaw in Shelby County, regards himself as an interpreter of universal religious trends.
>
> "What I see myself doing is trying to chronicle and illustrate what I believe is a budding spiritual renaissance emerging all over the world and

crossing all religions," Redfield said. "I'm trying to look at human culture and what people are moving to next."

After a recent poll, George Gallup said in all his years he has never seen such an interest in spirituality. The television network CNN (Dec. 15, 1999) conducted a survey of the large influx of films and TV programs on religious and spiritual themes, particularly Christian themes. Even Billy Graham, now in his eighties, attracts thousands of teenagers on his youth night during his evangelistic missions. All this is encouraging. And in August of 2000 Pope John Paul II called for a youth rally in Rome. To the amazement of all, more than two million young people traveled to Rome and stood for hours singing and hearing messages. More than 160 countries were represented. Spirituality is in. But attempting to reach postmoderns must be done wisely, understanding them and communicating Christ in a manner that is clear and satisfying.

The problem today for the church is complex because many postmoderns, or New Age advocates, reject the institutional church. For example, in a television interview on *Good Morning America* (ABC, May 17, 2000), Shirley MacLaine—a New Age advocate—told of a long 20-mile-a-day trek and said, "All you can think about is yourself, meaning, reality, etc." She went on, "Let the soul 'feel' you funnel in the divine. . . . Religious faith is different from spiritual faith. . . . Your soul, *not* the churches determine your fate." MacLaine epitomizes the spirit of the New Age postmodern when she urges us to look within ourselves to discover true spirituality. But Titus 3:4–7 states:

> But when the kindness of God our Savior and His love for mankind appeared, He saved us, not on the basis of deeds which we have done in righteousness, but according to His mercy, by the washing of regeneration and renewing by the Holy Spirit, whom He poured out upon us richly through Jesus Christ our Savior, so that being justified by His grace we might be made heirs according to the hope of eternal life.

Salvation is not in us; it's in Christ. The deeply disturbing fallout of this new milieu of the New Age in which people are trying to find spiritual meaning and value is that all people, whatever postmodern turn they may take, inevitably come face-to-face with their lostness, whether they will acknowledge it or not. They are lost to real purpose in life, lost to meaningful relationships, lost to themselves, *lost to God*. They float about on the turbulent sea of circumstances and conflicting ideologies, never able to settle in any port and discover reality. They actually are quite pessimistic in some respects, much like the older existentialists. To illustrate the point, look at the violence they face today in the schools.

Many question if they will survive ten more years. Homicide is the third largest killer among postmodern teenagers.

It is dramatically true that without Jesus Christ, all people are empty, estranged, and hopeless. Adrift on this turbulent postmodern sea, they desperately need to find anchor in Jesus Christ. This stands as objectively true and absolute in the twenty-first century as in the first. Apart from a saving relationship to God through Jesus Christ, postmoderns are profoundly and eternally lost. They need to find God and be redeemed from an empty life and an eternity of judgment.

Again, let it be stressed, the responsibility rests in the Christian community to direct people toward the only way of life that has meaning. That constitutes the church's prime task today. The problem is, as Shirley MacLaine stated, committed postmoderns do not normally look to the church for answers to their pressing problems. The statistics demonstrate that fact. The generational fallout in church attendance is reflected in the numbers:

40 percent of Builders go to church regularly

25 percent of Boomers go to church regularly

15 percent of Generation X go to church regularly

This is serious, and the church has responded to this situation in some rather strange ways.

Strange Reactions

The upheaval of society caused by the postmodern era has been met with widely divergent reactions within the thinking Christian community. There are those who consider any sort of reaction to traditional views a threat. Others want to do something to reach postmoderns but seem at a loss as to what to do. Then there are those who just shut their eyes and ears and plod along as usual. Surely these reactions are not the biblical answer and, therefore, no answer at all.

Conversely, New Age advocates herald the postmodern era as a day of liberation from old traditions, the demise of which is long overdue. Society has at last come of age and is free of any absolute worldview, especially a closed theological worldview. As Harvey Cox has said, "It is the loosing of the world from religious and quasi-religious understandings of itself, the dispelling of all closed world-views, the breaking of all supernatural myths and sacred symbols. . . . It has relativized religious world-views and thus rendered them innocuous."[12]

Such a situation leaves us uneasy because of the fact that a very basic question surfaces: Is the Christian worldview a valid presupposition (for it is a presupposition)? Can the Christian faith be convincingly defended? Again, a satisfying apologetic is demanded if we are to reach the postmodern New Age. This stands true because those adhering to the postmodern approach are by and large quite tolerant of other religions (especially Eastern religions) but seem negative to the Christian worldview with our commitment to absolutes. Is there an answer to this quandary? We must put that problem on the shelf until chapter 4 when the issue shall be discussed in more depth. Be all that as it may, it seems clear that an indefinite spirituality, which the postmodern wants, is not the biblical view and consequently will not give any lasting, satisfying answers to life's problems. The gospel of Jesus Christ alone stands as the answer. This is true for militant Islamics as well as for young postmoderns. All need Christ. The contemporary church must relate this truth to the entire world. Can it be done?

In this atmosphere the church is called on to minister. The task of the church is to present Christ to the world as we find it—not as it was or as we would like it to be—and to communicate in a relevant manner that in Christ alone can be found the only answer to life's ultimate questions. Here is where the trouble begins, for as implied above, it seems obvious that many churches have failed, at least to some extent, in their evangelistic responsibility. Moreover, it would appear that this relative ineffectiveness to communicate the gospel relevantly to a rapidly changing world is a growing problem, evidenced by the boycott of the institutionalized church by a growing segment of society. True, among postmoderns, there is a disillusionment with institutions in general and an overall questioning of everything that smacks of the Establishment. This applies not only to the younger postmoderns, but to the Boomer generation as well. Many churches have struggled with this spirit of rejection. As pointed out by Paul Musselman: "The dying urban churches are indication of an unplanned, but nevertheless real protest. . . . The stream of people who pass but never enter an urban church represents a form of unconscious picketing against the church."[13] But this disillusionment with institutionalism is not the only reason that people bypass churches today. Even national crises like terrorism and economic decay that bring more people to church—at least for a season—will not save the situation. There are two serious problems that cannot be disregarded, and we can do something constructive about them. These issues must be met courageously.

Two Issues to Face

First, the church's reluctance to change, update itself, and speak relevantly to our day constitutes a serious problem for more churches
than one. Let me illustrate this problematic attitude: I was once conducting a session on the theme of effective local church evangelism.
The participants came from different churches and consisted largely
of laypeople. I was advocating changes in programs and procedures
that would aid in more effectively reaching people with the gospel. In
the course of my many comments, I made one very minor, off-the-cuff
suggestion that perhaps we should look at the actual hour of Sunday
worship. It could be that meeting at a different hour would reach more
people. During the discussion period that followed, a layman suddenly
burst out, "What's wrong with meeting at eleven o'clock on Sunday
morning for worship?" Here was a man so bound to a specific time to
worship that he was angered at the thought of any change, even one as
minor as that. With this attitude, shared by many churchgoers, it's no
wonder that the radical change taking place in worship styles today is
causing disquietude.

When we speak of the necessity for overturning traditions, the reference is essentially to outmoded approaches and programs that fail to
reach a changing mind-set and culture. The great objective theologies
of Christianity must remain. The gospel itself is unchanging as shall be
discussed in a moment. But every generation has the right to hear the
Good News in a framework that addresses itself to them in their present sociological environment. This often implies change, perhaps drastic change at times. Georgia Harkness has rightly said, "If the church is
to win the battle against secularism by the sword of the Spirit, some
deep-seated changes are in order."[14] We can no longer conduct business
as usual. The business is the same, but conducting it as usual tends to
alienate multitudes without Christ. It is as simple as that. Granted, this
issue has been discussed ad nauseum, but the time for discussion is over.
Courageous action is now demanded. If we are in any way to meet the
demands of this revolutionary age, something of a counterrevolution
must take place within the churches. Let's not be a twenty-first-century
Rip Van Winkle. We can change significantly and become relevant if we
will.

Another impediment to the church's evangelistic ministry exerts itself
today. It centers in the somewhat uncertain sound, or irrelevant sound,
that some churches have trumpeted. Postmoderns hear the church's
message, but, probably because of their worldview, they are not convinced even if they understand it. Thus they lose confidence in the

church's claim to speak relevantly to their lives and they continue to do what is right (or wrong) in their own eyes. We do have good news. When that truth is heralded in an appropriate manner, people hear—even postmoderns. It is a message of power (Rom. 1:16), but we must be sure that our message is expressed in a way that people can understand and that leads them to grasp its validity. It must be contextualized. Our evangelism will never be successful until we declare the truth of Christ in a way that is relevant to postmoderns. They deserve to hear the truth presented in this way. We shall look at this essential principle more fully in chapter 3. But let's be relevant and communicate effectively the central truths of Jesus Christ.

Before considering in more detail how to evangelize effectively in the postmodern era, we must consider briefly our concept of what evangelism actually is and how the church must respond to its challenge. This is the subject of the next chapter.

Questions and Issues for Study

1. Define postmodernism.
2. What are its roots in previous philosophies and ideas?
3. How do you see it manifest itself in people today?
4. Give and discuss a classic case of a postmodern you know.
5. What are the basic errors of postmodernism?
6. What is good about this new spirit?
7. What principles must be learned to meet the postmodern perversions?
8. What aspect of the gospel strikes a responsive chord in the postmodern?
9. What are postmoderns *really* looking for?
10. How would you begin to communicate the message of Christ to postmoderns?

two

What Is Church-Centered Evangelism?

Various writers have at times used the term *evangelism* in a rather loose manner. A precise definition is important. We certainly need to be clear in our understanding of what the task actually is. In attempting to give a sound meaning to the term, an Anglican commission on evangelism wrote, "To evangelize is so to present Christ Jesus in the power of the Holy Spirit that men shall come to put their trust in God through Him, to accept Him as their Savior, and serve Him as their King in the fellowship of His church."[1]

W. E. Sangster, a Methodist, implied action as well as proclamation when he wrote: "Evangelism is going to the people outside. It is the proclamation of the good news of God in Jesus Christ to 'Them that are without.' . . . It is the sheer work of the herald. . . . He blows the trumpet and demands to be heard."[2]

D. T. Niles, a great missiologist, said that evangelism is "One beggar telling another beggar where to find bread."[3] This is how I define evangelism: Evangelism is a *concerted,* self-conscious *effort* to *confront* the unbeliever with the truth about and the claims of Christ with a view to *challenging* and *leading* that unbeliever into repentance toward God and faith in our Lord Jesus Christ and thus into the fellowship of his church that the discipleship process may carry on.

So there is our task: to evangelize a bewildered mass, caught up in a sociological, ethical, ecological, philosophical revolution that has all but overturned every stabilizing tradition. And the *entire church* must engage in the work. Moreover, the church must realize the necessity of framing the message in terms that the postmodern can grasp. As Robert Cunningham warned, "We are heading for sure disaster in the church of our contemporary society when we insist on forcing new wine into old wineskins."[4] Let me repeat: A new day is on us and, therefore, a new challenge lies before us. What a challenge it is! Will we win the day for Christ?

Now it must be said that the church still has a real measure of vitality; God can do mighty things through his people. We can evangelize our world in our generation if the whole church can be renewed, educated, and committed to the task. But for us to see this desperately needed renewal and a new dynamic impetus for outreach, it is essential that we first come to grips with our biblical theology. That is really where it all starts.

The Biblical Concept of Church-Centered Evangelism

Axiomatic is the fact that the first principle of church-centered evangelism revolves around the reality that outreach constitutes the church's *primary* mission in the world. Of course, the church engages in many activities to meet human needs, but outreach to a lost world makes up its essential and primary mission. This does not, however, state the case quite properly. The mission is actually God's mission. The church merely shares in the *missio Dei,* as it has been called. But in this secondary sense the church does have a calling and it has been commissioned to the task by our Lord himself. Surely all would agree that Jesus' statement in Matthew 28:19–20 is foundational to the very life and ministry of the church, and these words are clearly the words of evangelism: "Go forth therefore and make all nations my disciples; baptize men everywhere in the name of the Father and the Son and the Holy Spirit, and teach them to observe all that I have commanded you. And be assured, I am with you always, to the end of time" (NEB). Thus the church shares in the *missio Dei* and in so doing lives close to the heart of God.

It would seem that no apologetic is needed to convince the knowledgeable, biblical Christian that mission lies at the core of the local church's ministry. As Faris Whitesell tells us, "New Testament local churches were nerve centers of evangelism, and in this respect constitute a pattern for local churches of all ages. Missionary evangelism had produced these local churches, and they in turn made evangelism and missionary activity their main business."[5] Pastors and laypeople with insight have long recognized the scriptural truth that God expects the entire church to get involved in the task. As Leighton Ford has said, "If our goal is the penetration of the whole world; then for the agents to carry out the task we must aim at nothing less than the mobilization of the whole church."[6] And it stands true today. What will fully awaken the entire church from its traditional slumber and motivate it to fulfill its ministry? How will the average layperson be motivated and equipped? Wherein lies the means of awakening God's people to the plight of our postmodern era to do something about it?

Motivation

First, God's people must focus on the upheaval society is undergoing. This is why several pages were given to a diagnosis of this present postmodern scenario. It seems rather strange that some churches, themselves a part of society and to some extent thus sharing in the revolution, have developed something of a ghetto mentality. It seems correct to say the average church member really does not understand our postmodern revolution. All he or she seems to recognize is that things are not like they used to be and our church is not growing. Many years ago, the great Victorian preacher of London, Charles Haddon Spurgeon, put his finger on the perennial problem in his revolutionary day. It was a revolutionary day; the industrial revolution was at its height. Just before his death, Spurgeon preached:

> Oh, for a church of out-and-out believers, impervious to the soul-destroying doubt which pours upon us in showers!
>
> Yet all this would not reach our ideal. *We want a church of a missionary character,* which will go forth to gather out a people unto God from all parts of the world. A church is a soul-saving company, or it is nothing. If the salt exercises no preserving influence on that which surrounds it, what is the use of it? Yet some shrink from effort in their immediate neighbourhood because of the poverty and vice of the people. I remem-

ber a minister who is now deceased, a very good man he was, too, in many respects: but he utterly amazed me by a reply, which he made to a question of mine. I remarked that he had an awful neighbourhood round his chapel, and I said, "Are you able to do much for them?" He answered, "No, I feel almost glad that we keep clear of them; for, you see, if any of them were converted, it would be a fearful burden upon us." I knew him to be the soul of caution and prudence, but this took me aback, and I sought an explanation. "Well," he said, "we should have to keep them: they are mostly thieves and harlots, and if converted they would have no means of livelihood, and we are a poor people, and could not support them!" He was a devout man, and one with whom it was to one's profit to converse; and yet that was how he had gradually come to look at the case. His people with difficulty sustained the expenses of worship, and thus chill penury repressed a gracious zeal, and froze the genial current of his soul. There was a great deal of common sense in what he said, but yet it was an awful thing to be able to say it. We want a people who will not for ever sing,

> "We are a garden walled around,
> Chosen and made peculiar ground;
> A little spot enclosed by grace,
> Out of the world's wild wilderness."

It is good verse for occasional singing, but not when it comes to mean, "We are very few, and we wish to be." No, no brethren! We are a little detachment of the King's soldiers detained in a foreign country upon garrison duty; yet we mean not only to hold the fort, but to add territory to our Lord's dominion. We are not to be driven out; but, on the contrary, we are going to drive out the Canaanites; for this land belongs to us, it is given to us of the Lord, and we will subdue it. May we be fired with the spirit of discoverers and conquerors, and never rest while there yet remains a class to be rescued, a region to be evangelized!

We are rowing like lifeboat men upon a stormy sea, and we are hurrying to yonder wreck, where men are perishing. If we may not draw that old wreck to shore, we will at least, by the power of God, rescue the perishing, save life, and bear the redeemed to the shores of salvation. Our mission, like our Lord's, is to gather out the chosen of God from among men, that they may live to the glory of God. Every saved man should be, under God, a saviour: and the church is not in a right state until she has reached that conception of herself. The elect church is saved that she may save, cleansed that she may cleanse, blessed that she may bless. All the world is the field, and all the members of the church should work therein for the great Husbandman. Waste lands are to be reclaimed, and forests broken up by the plough, till the solitary place begins to blossom as the rose. We must not be content with holding our own: we must invade the territories of the prince of darkness.[7]

Spurgeon was right. Until the church becomes aware of the contemporary cultural scene and realizes that God's commission centers on ministering in a preserving capacity to that real world out there, it will experience difficulty in becoming the "church for others." As the report of the Western European Working Group of the Department on Studies in Evangelism of the World Council of Churches aptly pointed out:

> Faced with secular society, with the understanding of history as involving constant change and transformation and with the acknowledgement that the Church has to turn itself outwards to the world, we are summoned in the present age, as in any age. The church always stands in danger of perpetuating come-structures instead of replacing them by go-structures. One may say that inertia has replaced the dynamism of the Gospel and of participation in the mission of God. . . . Because of this inertia and this insulation from the world, we have come to exist beside and often outside the reality of the world, instead of being present in its structures. Our own structures then operate as obstacles and hindrances preventing the proclamation of the Gospel from reaching mankind.[8]

Despite the difficulties, the church must stand in the gap and minister Christ to the world. And we must not give in to despair for the contemporary church; it can rise to the challenge of the postmodern hour. The Holy Spirit constantly moves God's people toward renewal and resurrection, and there are many signs that point in the direction of renewal today, for instance, a fresh interest in evangelism everywhere, ministers gathering in conferences and clinics on outreach, new evangelistic thrusts developing in various church groups, a growing awareness of the need, and above all a deeper commitment to prayer than seen for many years. All these dynamics should encourage those committed to evangelism. Hopefully we will rise to the occasion and see a new worldwide gospel impact.

Still, difficult days lie ahead. The church is not going to be revolutionized inwardly so as to cope with the revolution outside until some forthright and courageous challenge is presented to it. And from what quarter will such a call and challenge come? It seems self-evident from what quarter it *should* come, namely, the pastor, teachers, and church leadership. It would seem vital for the informed layperson as well as for the minister and leaders of the congregation to realize that in church-centered evangelism the leaders play the key role.

The Responsibility of the Pastor and Leaders as Evangelists

This theme immediately brings to mind Paul's challenge to Timothy to "do the work of an evangelist" (2 Tim. 4:5). By clear implication in this passage, the pastor and/or leader cannot fulfill his or her God-given role unless he or she assumes the evangelist's place. This certainly means more than merely preaching evangelistic sermons or teaching on the theme from time to time, although that constitutes a part of it. In the light of the Scriptures and in a day like today, it means leading the entire church to become alive to people—postmoderns and moderns alike—and to grow an evangelistic and mission-minded body. Experience has surely taught us, as C. E. Autrey puts it:

> The place of the pastor in the evangelism of the local church is strategic. If he is evangelistic, the church will ordinarily be evangelistic. The degree to which the pastor is evangelistic will be reflected in the church. If he is lukewarm, the church will very likely be lukewarm. If he is intensely evangelistic, the church will reflect the warmth and concern of the pastor.[9]

Autrey is on target; a local church eventually takes on the basic spiritual attitudes of its pastor and leaders of the various aspects of church life. This is as it should be if any leader's ministry is at all effective. Therefore, the essential principle of the leader becoming in a true sense an evangelist cannot be overstated. If a local church aspires to be an evangelistic church and geared to effective outreach, the pastor and leaders become the key persons in evangelizing their day and time. For example, how will the average church member ever learn to evangelize the postmoderns of our society if the pastor and leaders do not inform, teach, and lead them into such a ministry? This is a basic, biblical principle, so basic one would think it not necessary to stress, but it must be strongly emphasized.

The Leader-Evangelist

It can be asked, of course, is the leader's role really that of an evangelist? Has the case been overstated? The answer can be found in what the New Testament presents as the position of the pastor and leaders in a particular local congregation. It must first be recognized that today, in all denominations, we are probably not duplicating in every detail the New Testament pattern concerning the administrative leadership of the churches. For example, there was a plurality of elders or pastors, which only the large contemporary churches have. Moreover, the bishop had a somewhat different role than the present-day bishop in those communions that still keep the office. It seems that the Bible appears somewhat flexible on church structures. The point is, however, the New Testament words that are used to describe the various offices in the first-century church present something of an insight into the function of today's pastor. And in a limited sense, the principles relate to the various local church leaders.

Look first at the word translated "presbyters" or "elders." This term is essentially a title of dignity. The early church borrowed it from the Jewish community. Members of the honored Sanhedrin, for example, were often called elders. It seems that the Greeks also used the term in a similar fashion before the Jewish community brought it into their vocabulary. The actual function of the dignified office of elder is found in the word *episkopoi,* translated "bishop," literally meaning "overseer." Joseph Thayer points out, "that they (the elders) did not differ at all from the *(episkopoi)* bishop or overseer (as is acknowledged also by Jerome on Titus 1:5) . . . is evident from the fact that the two words are used indiscriminately. . . . The title *episkopos* denotes the function, *presbuteros* the dignity."[10]

These leaders, as the terms imply, served as the "governing" body of the local church. That governing role was granted by the Holy Spirit to lead and equip the church in its ministry. They were charged with the task of leading the congregation into a proper life and spiritual experience of Christ in service. Paul makes it crystal clear that the Holy Spirit made them overseers (Acts 20:28), and they were "to shepherd" *(poimainein)* the church of God. But this office was not only one of authority, though it certainly was that.

In James we find these leaders visiting and praying for the sick (James 5:13–15). In 1 Timothy 5:17 the elders are to "labour in the word and doctrine" (KJV). Hebrews 13:7, 17, 24 (though another Greek word is used for the office of elder) states that those who rule are those who "have spoken unto you the word of God"; and, for the sake of the readers, "watch for your souls" (KJV). This combination of ruling with preaching, teaching, and assuming pastoral responsibility clearly lines up with the entire New Testament concept of the leadership ministry. Most keenly to be felt by the ministers was their responsibility to God for the welfare of the flock under their charge.

Another aspect of ministry is found in the Greek word *diakonoi,* i.e., "deacon" or "servant." Although there seems to be a special group of leaders in the New Testament churches who were appointed to this particular office and ministry, the word is used at times interchangeably with the positions of elder, evangelist, or even apostle (see 1 Cor. 3:5). Well-known is the fact that the word essentially means "service" or "ministering." And as again found in Thayer, the term is often used in connection with those who, "by God's command, promote and proclaim religion among men."[11] The prime impact of this word centers in the fact that the chief function of God's servant becomes ministering to God's people to promote the true faith of Christ. The form and mode of service can take various avenues of ministry.

One of the most interesting passages concerning the leadership ministry in the New Testament church is that found in Ephesians 4:11–12. "And these were his gifts: some to be apostles, some prophets, some evangelists, some pastors and teachers, to equip God's people for work in his service, to the building up of the body of Christ" (NEB). These verses clearly present the office-bearers of the first-century church and give insight into the organization and administrative structure of the early congregations. William Barclay states from this Ephesian passage that three kinds of office-bearers arose in Paul's time. (1) There were those whose authority and word were universal, that is to the entire church. (2) There were also those whose ministry was not restricted to one place. They had a wandering or itinerant ministry. (3) Finally, there were those who ministered essentially to one congregation in one place.[12]

In the first category of ministry we find the apostles. This meant more than just the Twelve. For instance, Silvanus (1 Thess. 1:1; 2:6), Andronicus and Junias (Rom. 16:7), and of course Paul and Barnabas were called apostles in the sense that the term is used in Ephesians 4. It was required that these leaders had seen the Lord and been a witness to his resurrection. In this historical sense, this specific office was to pass away. Yet in spirit, all true leaders are apostles, for they are the "ones sent" *(apostolos)* by God to bear witness to the resurrection.

The second group of ministers, the "wanderers," are called prophets and evangelists. The prophet, as a forth-teller (more than a foreteller) of God's truth, went about sharing Christ in the power of the Spirit and was a person of great influence. It appears that this *official* office vanished from the life of the early church. Perhaps there were those who abused the role so that it fell into disrepute. Yet the "gift of prophecy" exists to this day. The evangelists were probably what we today would call missionaries, as well as itinerant declarers of the gospel. They were the heralds of good news. So in principle, the two offices continue. In the first century they did not exercise the prestige or authority of the apostles; they were more or less the rank-and-file missionaries and prophets of the church who went about proclaiming God's truth.

Finally, there were the pastor-teachers. They were the more settled and permanent ministry leaders in the local church. This office title seems to be a double phrase to describe one essential group of leaders and ministers. Their task is found in their title; they were to teach and preach, and the content of their message was the Christian faith. These servants of the local church were more than simply teachers and preachers; they were also what we today would understand as pastoral leaders *(poimenas)* or shepherds. They were commissioned to feed the flock of God (1 Peter 5:2) and to care for and protect the sheep (Acts 20:28). Jesus Christ himself is the supreme example, for he is called the Chief Shepherd (1 Peter 5:4) and the Shepherd of all our souls (1 Peter 2:25). What a responsible position! As Barclay says, "The shepherd of the flock of God . . . feeds them with the truth, . . . seeks them when they stray away, and . . . defends them from all that would hurt or destroy or distort their faith."[13]

The impact of this Ephesians passage for our present purpose is not merely to present a picture of the New Testament structures of the ministry, interesting as it may be. What should be grasped centers in the fact that God selected these special leaders as his gifts to the church so that all his people might be equipped to do the work of the ministry. As has already been emphasized, the whole church has been commissioned to the ministry. The "ministers" or "leaders" as we may call them are given to the church to prepare the church to carry on its service.

The impact of this well-known and much discussed principle in the field of evangelism is obvious. Having discovered that the prime ministry of the church centers in mission, the clear implication is that the real evangelists are the church members themselves. The pastor and leaders fill their role in equipping the believers under their charge for this vital task. Drawing this conclusion cannot be avoided when one considers all that the New Testament declares concerning the leaders of a congregation and the place they fill relative to mission. They are bishops, overseers, elders, leaders of respect and honor; they are deacons, servants of the people; and they are pastors, those who feed and guard the flock. They are prophets, who are sent by God to speak in the power of the Holy Spirit; they are evangelists who herald good news. This is something of the spirit and responsibility of pastors and leaders as they attempt to lead the flock of God with spiritual authority into fields of evangelistic service.

This constitutes a fantastic order, and no one person can possibly possess all of these gifts to perfection. Yet surely the leaders in a local congregation can assume the basic responsibility of leading and equipping the whole church to fulfill its ministry. Into this position the Holy Spirit has called them, and regardless of how inadequate they may feel—or actually may be—for this work, they must unreservedly give themselves as best they can.

So we come back to the previous theme: the entire church becoming mobilized and equipped to evangelize our revolutionary postmodern society. And it should be amply clear that the essential responsibility for this Herculean task of leading and equipping the church to rise to the challenge settles essentially on the shoulders of the pastors and leaders. As stated by Whitesell:

> The Pastor-evangelist, then, is the man in local church evangelism, and local church evangelism is the key to all other evangelism. The pastor must lead . . . people in intercessory prayer for the lost; inspire them, teach them, organize them, send them out, and encourage them to continue in this greatest of all church work.[14]

This then makes up the leader's task, and it is not putting it too strongly to say that if he or she fails in this obligation, the leader has missed a very vital part of ministry.

Examples of Leader-Evangelists

History is not without its examples to reinforce the validity of the leader-evangelist principle. Take the marvelous ministry of Richard Baxter of Kidderminster, England, in the eighteenth century. Although he served as pastor in a small town of only five thousand and came to a very provincial and weak church, he was soon used by the Spirit of God to kindle a bright flame of evangelism. Baxter was an exceptionally powerful preacher; he "preached as a dying man to dying men," he said. He also did much personal evangelism. So committed was he to the task, that he visited every family in the community. But perhaps his greatest genius lay in the fact that he led his people to set up family worship in their homes where they could communicate the Christian faith to their families and others. As a result of the remarkable work of Baxter as a pastor-evangelist, it has been said that "Kidderminster became a veritable colony of heaven in an hour of general spiritual darkness and wickedness."[15]

Or look at the ministry of Charles Haddon Spurgeon in the last century. We all know him as a preacher par excellence. Still, he devoted a large part of his ministry to the training of young men to go out and share Christ. Spurgeon once said, "He who converts a soul draws water from a fountain, but he who trains a soul-winner digs a well, from which thousands may drink to eternal life." And he realized the principle of the entire church being enlisted in the task. In the previously quoted inaugural address, he said:

> In some "the church" signifies the ministers or clergy; but in truth it should signify the whole body of the faithful, and there should be an opportunity for these to meet together to act as a church. It is, I judge, for the church of God to carry on the work of God in the land. The final power and direc-

tion is with our Lord Jesus, and under Him it should lie, not with some few who are chosen by delegation or by patronage, but with the whole body of believers. We must more and more acknowledge the church, which God has committed to our charge; and in so doing, we shall evoke a strength, which else lies dormant. If the church is recognized by Christ Jesus, it is worthy to be recognized by us; for we are the servants of the church.[16]

And space precludes the interesting accounts of giants of the past who spent much time training evangelists to declare Christ, leaders like John Wesley, Charles Finney, William and Catherine Booth, Bernard of Clairvaux, Francis of Assisi, and a host of others. When we come to our day and time, we can find clear examples of the leader-evangelist at work. I know of a pastor who excelled in his responsibility in this field. He started his work with two concerned laymen. He taught and encouraged them in the area of personal evangelism. These two men began to lead people to faith in Christ. Soon they recruited two more to join them in the work. Now four men were engaged. Soon there were eight as the work developed. Before long women were inspired, and they along with several young people gave themselves to the task. Soon a host of trained and zealous Christians, men and women alike, were constantly witnessing. The consequences are that many were reached for Christ. It took time to be sure, but here was a leader who saw his role and took it seriously. Starting with only two men, working with them and training them for mission, he became a pastor-evangelist in a most profound sense.

Many more examples could be cited, but these given make it quite clear that any church can come alive to its opportunity of the challenging hour if the pastor and leadership will take up the challenge and lead the people of God in becoming aware of today's mind-set, and teach them how to share the gospel intelligently. This ministry the Spirit of God honors and uses.

Now it may sound somewhat idealistic to make such claims; many may even feel it impossible to mobilize an entire congregation. And granted, the ideal may never be perfectly realized. But regardless of the problems, the principle remains and the obligation must be faced by pastors and leaders. In chapter 5 we shall be discussing this theme in far more detail and will attempt to present some practical ideas wherein a solid beginning can perhaps be found.

Conclusion

The inevitable conclusion of all that has been said is quite simple. The major premise is that the evangelization of our turbulent, changing, postmodern world rests on the challenging, educating, and equipping of the whole body of Christ to engage in the *missio Dei*. The minor premise is that this equipping task is essentially the responsibility of the pastor and various leaders in the local congregation. If the mission is to be significantly successful, the pastor and leaders must rise to the challenge of their roles. If they fail and refuse to become in a very profound sense evangelists, the church will suffer. But if they do rise to the hour, the church can awake from its slumber and pick up the task of the day. And this is the task a postmodern world waits to see. But how do we get a hearing from this new postmodern worldview? That becomes the next imperative topic to explore.

Questions and Issues for Study

1. What constitutes the essential meaning of evangelism?
2. What role does evangelism play in God's mission in the world?
3. What role does evangelism play in the responsibility of the local church?
4. Who is to be involved in the evangelistic task and why?
5. Who is responsible for equipping the church to evangelize, and what role do they play?
6. How can the local church rise to the challenge of evangelism?
7. How do the various "leaders" fulfill their respective leadership roles?
8. Can the "average" layperson truly evangelize? How?
9. What is the role of the Holy Spirit in the task of evangelism?
10. What place does the Word of God have in evangelism?

three

Having an Answer
to Postmodern Questions

The Bible declares beyond doubt that Christians are to witness for Jesus Christ. Our Lord said, "You shall be My witnesses" (Acts 1:8). That leaves the church no options. But sharing the good news of Christ is not always a comfortable exercise, especially when one meets a postmodern skeptic who has serious doubts concerning the faith and raises arguments against Christianity. To speak of one's faith with those predisposed to listen with an open mind can be exhilarating, but the listener with a skeptical mind creates another situation entirely. Yet we cannot escape or evade the call to communicate Christ to all, even to the serious critic. The Scriptures state we are to be always "ready to make a defense to *everyone* who asks you to give an account for the hope that is in you" (1 Peter 3:15, italics added). That means we must be *prepared* to witness, perhaps especially to the doubting postmodern.

That unavoidable assignment is formidable indeed. How can we "always be ready" to share Christ, especially as we face an increasingly questioning age? We need resources if we hope to witness intelligently and convincingly. This is vital if we are to point others to faith in the Lord Jesus Christ.

The purpose of this chapter is to present in capsule form some sensible answers to the skeptic's questions and convincing reasons for believing in and receiving Christ as Lord and Savior. Christians need to provide answers. Postmoderns must be led to see the truth and wisdom of the gospel if we are to help them find Christ. Since God expects more of his people than simply winning an argument, we are to present Christ as the One who can truly meet a person's needs and give an abundant life now and for eternity (John 10:10). The love of Christ demands such an approach. These facts surface a real need for the effective witness.

The Need

The church today demands concerned Christians who possess some expertise in presenting helpful answers to the arguments against their faith, that is, believers who are able to offer some cogent reasons for what they believe. If people choose to ignore or reject the truth of Christ after being confronted with the reasonableness of Christianity, then they bear the responsibility; but they have the right to hear a coherent presentation of the faith. That puts the burden on us who do believe. Our responsibility centers in helping unbelievers work through their doubts to faith. If the church fails in such a call, we are to that extent culpable for this generation's rejection of Christ. Therefore, we must take up the gauntlet and try to answer whatever doubts or skepticism separate unbelievers from a saving knowledge of Jesus Christ. So the question becomes: How do we believers carry out our responsibility as defenders and apologists for the faith?

It should be understood at the outset that answering doubting postmoderns involves knowing not only what to say but *how to say it*. Therefore, before examining several specific arguments of the skeptic and presenting a suggested Christian answer, we must carefully consider how to approach the postmodern.

In the first place, a Christian must pray for God's guidance, patience, and understanding. Anyone who would communicate Christ effectively must do it in the wisdom, power, and love of the Spirit. Mere argumentation rarely convinces or wins anyone. That is especially true if a person is closed minded or if his or her doubts are not truly honest; argumentation will rarely touch or move that person. And such is often the case today. Postmoderns tend to retreat into some sort of abstraction that all truth—including religious moral absolutes—is relative. Many thus reject Christ because they prefer to remain in sin and refuse the leadership of Jesus in their lives. Our Lord said of his contemporaries: "Light from heaven came into the world, but they loved the darkness more than the Light, for their deeds were evil. They hated the heavenly Light because they wanted to sin in the darkness. They stayed away from that Light for fear their sins would be exposed and they would be punished" (John 3:19–20 TLB). The problem of clinging to sin (darkness) rather than repenting and turning to Christ (light) should be dealt with forthrightly, but if people are honest in their doubts, believers can many times help them to faith. Through God's guidance and loving patience, a way can often be found into the heart, mind, and soul of the *sincere* skeptic.

Moreover, Christ's incarnation, "God with us," is far more than a mere theological proposition; it is a principle to be understood and applied to one's own life. As Christ became flesh to reach out and save sinners, we must exemplify the same spirit of self-giving. To impact others, a willingness to identify with them in the spirit of the incarnation is vital. The challenge for all Christians centers in giving ourselves to the lost, just as Jesus did. Love wins most arguments.

To identify with and witness to the questioning postmodern will not be easy, however. Paul Tournier describes the problem: "Listen to the conversations of the world. They are for the most part dialogues of the deaf. A person speaks in order to set forth his own ideas, in order to justify himself, in order to enhance himself."[1] Is that what people see in the witnessing of Christians? Hopefully not! We must be willing to listen and empathize with people. We are not in the business of just unloading the gospel on people "to get it off our chest" and relieve our own guilt for not witnessing enough. Paul Tournier knows that communicating effectively with people requires sensitivity in which one identifies with "the innumerable throng of men and women laden down with their secrets, fears, suffering, sorrows, disappointments and faults."[2]

To reach doubters we must become genuinely concerned for them as people whom God loves. Christians do have helpful answers to their questions, but before they will receive them, they must know that we love them and accept them as people created in God's image and for whom Christ died. If we keep the fact that Christ died for them paramount in our minds, we will discover that we can learn to care for even the most adamant anti-Christian. The principle is plain: People are reached primarily through love. We learn to "argue" well because we love well. So take courage; the church can respond to skeptical postmoderns. There are many apologetic answers to the doubts of contemporary people, which we will now consider.

The Humanistic Postmodern

What lies behind many doubts concerning the claims of Christ? That constitutes the prime question. Seen from the spiritual perspective, the old battle of satanic deception rages on. Coupled with human sin, the prince of darkness blinds the minds of those who do not believe (2 Cor. 4:3). From the *human* perspective it is just that—*humanism*.

The spirit of humanism in one form or another has been with us for eons. Postmoderns did not invent it, even though many have given themselves to its precepts. Actually, it started in the Garden of Eden when Adam and Eve were expelled, and it has run through the course of history to the contemporary moment. To oversimplify, as pointed out earlier, the humanistic worldview declares the final source of all truth and meaning in life is found in one's own self. The criteria of all things rest in the human. For the postmodern today, humanism manifests itself in forms such as the denial of external absolutes: "What suits me is okay"; "We are our own judges"; "We must save ourselves"; and so on. This humanistic spirit is integrated into all of life, including ethics, morals, religion, and one's attitude toward the gospel of Christ.

It must be acknowledged that this humanistic approach to life often asks the right question. The humanist raises issues like, How can life be filled with meaning? That is a commendable query and should be asked by all. However, the postmodern's answer is that meaning is found in oneself, and this presents a real problem as we declare that Christ is the answer to the quest for meaning. For the humanistic worldview, Christ is *not* the answer; we are. Believers must recognize the force of this humanistic approach.

Modern Versions of the Error

More than a few college professors today, and many others, teach and hold that this new humanistic spirit is the religion of the hour and surely of tomorrow. They say historic conservative Christianity may be all right for those who want it, but it is far from mandatory for all, as no absolute criteria exists for ultimate truth and reality. Spirituality is great, they argue, but we all can seek it in our own humanistic way. And the fact that they have been heard and heeded by many appears obvious. Sociological data tell us that these concepts are affecting our contemporary society more than any other value system or philosophical worldview at the contemporary moment.

Humanist Manifesto, written years ago but still revered by many, states, "Traditional religions . . . inhibit humans from helping themselves or experiencing their full potentialities."[3] Committed humanists hold that what "satisfies" them is fine, no matter what others may see as true. Karl Marx expressed the central concept well when he argued, "The root of mankind is man, not God."[4] Many have bought into this philosophical worldview. This presents a serious issue, and Christians are called to react, but we must be careful not to overreact. The situation should not so disturb us that we respond to the postmodern challenge in an un-Christian or careless manner. On the other hand, we cannot afford to underreact. We need to understand this enemy of Christianity.

With the postmodern's denial of absolutes, which is really the issue of humanism, such a worldview can easily degenerate into a lifestyle of low morality. For example, Dr. Mary Calderone, 1974 Humanist of the Year, stated that teenagers should experiment with sex and that extramarital sex may be good for people. She declared, "An extramarital affair that's really solid might have very good results."[5] Of course not all postmoderns ascribe to that level of sexual morality, but their state is still sad indeed.

Many postmoderns are like the people described in the tower of Babel story (Genesis 11). Here a people had lost their relationship with God, so they decided to create their own human-centered spirituality and prove their greatness by building a tower that would reach high into the Mideast sky. It would be a super tower built by super people and thus solidify and unify their super society. As one biblical scholar points out, when they had lost their faith in God, they realized that they needed something to keep them united; therefore, they created their own spirituality, symbolized by the tower of Babel.

Their new world, however, never came off. The tower of Babel became the symbol of division and chaos. No one can build a satisfying lifestyle or viable society on a mere humanistic foundation. The unpleasant surprise for the present-day tower of Babel builders centers in the fact that the end results are far from what was expected. Of course, personal material needs may be taken care of, and that is important and good. But are the people better off morally with postmodernism and its denial of absolutes than they would be with Christianity? Are they happier? Does life have more meaning? The answers are found in the fact that the suicide rate for teenagers is appalling. Recent statistics tell us it is one of the highest causes of teenage deaths. And that is not to mention the violence that has erupted in our schools. MTV does not create a meaningful life.

Granted, all postmoderns do not plunge into amoralism, but many do. Their basic worldview tends to promote it. And when we sow to the wind, we reap the whirlwind (Hosea 8:7). We, as faithful witnesses, must point these things out to the inquiring mind.

But there is still a big hurdle in commending Christianity to people of this mind-set. Although they may to some degree be attracted by what Christianity appears to offer, they have difficulty believing that a revelational faith can be absolutely true and reliable and thus able to deliver on its claims. That is to say, they question the truth and demands of Jesus Christ. They have a problem accepting that the *only* true source of genuine spirituality is Jesus Christ. The issue of absolutes rears its head again. What can the witness for Christ then say?

An Answer

The first issue is to help postmoderns recognize that absolutes do actually exist. To say there are no absolutes denies reality. The physical laws of gravity, the consistency of mathematics, the reliability of our sense perception, and so on demonstrate absolutes. But what about Einstein's theories of relativity? He told us even time and space are relative to the speed of the observer. And Einstein was correct. Time and space are relative; they are not "absolutes" in themselves. They vary according to the speed of the one who perceives them. As one approaches the speed of light, if that were possible, time slows down and space collapses. The old world of Sir Isaac Newton no longer exists with its concept of absolute space and time. If one is moving slowly, as we do on earth, the Newtonian world of rigid time, space, and gravity works, but not if one is traveling at 186,000 miles per second, the speed of light. And Einstein's theory is no longer a theory. It is demonstrable in the cosmological laboratory.

So, the postmoderns may argue, if there are no absolutes in the entirety of the created universe, how can there be any absolutes in any sphere of thought? Did Einstein really eliminate absolutes? No, definitely not. A noted scientific writer Nigel Colder of Great Britain has pointed this out in his masterful work on Einstein:

> Albert Einstein did not cut adrift all the pieces of the universe to wander vaguely through ill-defined space and time. While he abolished the framework of absolute space and absolute time he replaced them by absolute space-time. Although a more malleable kind of thing than its predecessors it is, if anything, more reliably absolute. Newtonian space and time

were like a chessboard on which the game of matter and energy was played. Einsteinian space-time takes an active part in the game and may even be regarded as being created by energy. At any rate, it shares fully in the history and fate of the contents of the universe. Among the paraphernalia of relativity theory, the speed of light is absolute, the pattern of curved space near a massive object is absolute, the rest-energy of an object is absolute. And all the laws of physics are absolute. . . . they are consistent throughout the universe.[6]

In other words, the entire universe operates on absolutes. To say there are no absolutes denies the very nature of the universe itself.

Our conclusion then is that absolutes absolutely do exist at the very core of all reality. The postmodern argument falls to the ground. Some things are just absolutely true. Einstein has proved it. And if such is the case in the physical universe, how true it must therefore be in other realms as well, especially in spirituality and morality, which are far more important than the physical. That just stands to reason. Help the postmodern see this obvious conclusion. This is an important and cogent argument for the absolute truth of the gospel.

A Practical Conclusion and Approach

To compliment the postmodern for his or her interest, even concern, for spirituality is often a wise first step. Be positive. Then point out that in light of the fact that there are, in principle, absolutes in the very fabric of reality, there surely must be absolute spiritual truth that will satisfy and create a full, rich, meaningful life. To repeat the principle, if the physical universe is made up of absolute principles, the spiritual realm, which far supersedes in importance the physical, surely has its absolutes. That is only reasonable. It follows quite naturally. The law of noncontradiction still works. Furthermore, one cannot really live, even in our "slow" Newtonian world, and ignore absolutes. A crude illustration makes the point. A bus racing down the street is absolutely there. Do not step in its path. If you do, you're dead. That is absolutely true. Even to say there are absolutely no absolutes is to create one. Point these things out to postmoderns. Tell them about Jesus Christ. Share who he is, what he promises, and what he did on the cross and in his resurrection to make those promises viable. Simply put, communicate the gospel. These are the absolutes that "work." Paul was right when he declared that the gospel truth is absolute and the power of God for salvation (Rom. 1:16). Knock down that straw man who says absolutes do not exist, and then let God do his work. Christ can speak for himself. He truly did come into this world that one might have life and have it more abundantly (John 10:10). That is an absolute spiritual and historical truth and will communicate to those of an open mind as we attempt to tear down their humanistic hope in their personal tower of Babel. After all, that tower is only a tower of sin that ultimately falls in ruin.

Thus Christ and the biblical gospel make sense. Faith is not a blind leap into the dark. The person willing to acknowledge his or her sin and need of Jesus Christ—that is, honestly face absolute reality—will always find him. The Scriptures are powerful indeed and reveal God's truth. The Bible declares absolute truth. We shall argue this case shortly. Of course, as stressed, no one is ever brought to Christ by mere argument alone. Yet we are to always be ready to make a defense, and in that context, present Christ. All apologetics—a defense for the faith—can do is knock down false barriers and hopefully open the door for a presentation of the gospel. Today that is important, and the church must be equipped to do it.

A New Deist View

More than one postmodern, with their appreciation of "spirituality," would agree with Voltaire (1694–1778), the philosopher who said, "I believe in God, not the God of the mystics and the theologians, but the God of nature, the great geometrician, the architect of the universe, the prime mover, unalterable, transcendental, everlasting."[7] A professor writing to a minister friend stated, "There are scads of students I have discovered on our university campuses that believe in a 'force' beyond it all, but a quite impersonal 'force.'"

One of the largest groups of present-day doubters of Christianity are those who believe in God but only in a nonpersonal way. They see him as a great force, the creator of all, perhaps even in some sense a "personality." Somewhat reminiscent of Eastern thought, they accept spirituality, but God is grasped as far removed from the dynamic of personal daily life. Such types are found everywhere, but especially on college and high school campuses and among younger teenagers. They see themselves as very modern and up-to-date, but their position is no more than a modern version of old-line deism.

Before we attempt any response to this mind-set, it will help to examine the position of a famous, historical figure of that type. Understanding him may aid us in comprehending his contemporary counterparts and help us develop an answer for them.

François-Marie Arouet may not be a readily recognizable name unless we mention his nickname—Voltaire. He was born in Paris and died there eighty-three years later. He became a startling and satirical spokesman for a spirit that has seriously challenged historical Christianity. What was the approach that Voltaire so ardently espoused? In *A Handbook of Theological Terms*, Van A. Harvey defines it as "the view that regards God as the intelligent creator of an independent and law-abiding world but denies that He providentially guides it or intervenes in any way with its course of destiny."[8] Although embracing a vague belief in God, Voltaire believed that he is merely a great, creative force, having no actual involvement in the earthly affairs of life. D. Elton Trueblood explains: "How easy it is to use the word 'God' and mean very little is shown vividly by the history of . . . deistic . . . belief. . . . Though the term is now seldom used, a great deal of what passes for belief today is sheer deism and nothing more and is, therefore, woefully inadequate."[9]

Voltaire personified deism in his day. A man of profound influence, he was far more committed to rationalistic modernity than most post-moderns, but his view of God seems much like that of many in our hour. His approach lingers on. A number of young people and others believe in an impersonal, uninvolved God. They are for justice and reason, even spirituality in a vague sense, but they reject a personal experience of an involved God and any form of personal revelational truth. Consequently, and not surprisingly, their image of God has been reduced to that of an ill-defined force or intelligence that has nothing to do with practical, everyday life on earth. And that is exactly where the problem lies.

This position leaves us with a God, who, in the final analysis, is not really God at all. This highest Being—though he may have created this vast universe and have some sort of personality—in twenty-first-century terminology is little more than a cosmological computer creator. Since modern deists do not grant God involvement in daily affairs, his personality does not really matter in the dynamics of anyone's personal life. God is an "impersonal personality," if there can be such a thing.

An Answer

Clearly such a "God" as the deists propose lacks the highest divine attribute known to us—involved personality. This deistic concept of God is hardly tenable. Personality in its full sense is central to all meaningful experience. How then could the highest of human concepts, personhood (and that surely implies involvement in other personalities), be denied in the highest reality—a creating God? We, the creation, as humans, are persons of involvement with others. How could he, our Creator, be less? A creator could hardly create a higher order than himself. It is radically inconsistent. Trueblood targets this untenable end result, saying, "There is a fundamental absurdity in supposing that the God in whom he believes is inferior to himself in the *order of being*. If God is a mere 'power,' and not a center of consciousness, then I, the humble creature, am actually superior, in a very important way to the Creator."[10] In other words, the uninvolved Creator is inferior to his creation because of his uninvolved personhood. That does not make sense. How can God be God at all if he is not a personal, loving, forgiving, redeeming, involved Person?

In the final analysis this approach ends in a theology almost totally devoid of God, and that simply is not a meaningful theology at all. We must help the postmodern who has embraced this position see its fatal weakness. Of course, not all postmoderns hold this view of God and spirituality. Many have a more personal view of God. But an element of the group, at least for all practical purposes, understands God in this way. We must attempt to help them see the inconsistency of their position and how God involved himself dynamically in every human life when Christ, God's Son, came, lived, died, and rose again to recreate fallen mankind in his own image. That is Good News indeed.

The Self-Sufficient Postmodern

Friedrich Nietzsche boasted of himself as a skeptical thinker of the first magnitude. Through the last one hundred years, multitudes have been influenced and conditioned by his thought, even if they do not realize it or accept the more radical aspects of his ideas. Why does he attract so many? The answer is quite simple: He was a visionary advocate of becoming a self-sufficient, strong-willed person. And he saw this worldview as the necessary antidote to being a "meek Christian." Like many of his age, and ours, he became intrigued and inspired by what Charles Darwin theorized as "the survival of the fittest." He was determined to achieve aggressive self-sufficiency through *the will to power*. That approach has always had its appeal, even as it does today.

Nietzsche's philosophical travels led him up the primrose path and actually into an insane asylum. He was cared for by his mother, who nursed him until she died. Then his sister took over. The promoter of the concept of a self-made person came full circle. He had struggled long and hard through his own personal power to break away from the beliefs, values, and what he termed the "meekness" of his life, only to end up powerless and under the care of his Christian mother and sister. The philosophical prodigal son was brought home by those who loved him, and they displayed a quiet, compassionate strength, emanating from their faith in God.

During his prime, Nietzsche contemptuously condemned the faith of his family. He was convinced that growing up and becoming a real self meant cutting himself off from parental rules and regulations (sounds like some postmoderns today). A part of this for Nietzsche involved severing the religious ties of the past that bound him to biblical truths and principles. He strove to be a man of faith, not in God but totally in his human self, like the humanists.

Nietzsche used three words to describe what he conceived as the greatest event of history, three words that have become his most famous, or infamous, statement: "God is dead."[11] He no longer needed God; he was free. Self-sufficiency was attained. God was gone—dead. In one sense, this was humanism at its extreme. He became an outright atheist, and that constitutes a unique brand of humanism pushed to the limit.

Although scores of our contemporary postmoderns may not be as cavalier as Nietzsche, a basic self-sufficient attitude often characterizes them. "Do your own thing" has become the motto of many, God notwithstanding. Self-sufficiency can precipitate a practical atheism. For such, God may well be dead, as far as the pragmatic matters of life are concerned.

Nietzsche, the radical, argued that "the man of faith, the believer, is necessarily a small type of man."[12] In his opinion, such a person is bound to a "slave morality" (Christian ethics) that stifles human freedom and self-development. Thus he urged his followers to become "supermen," to become people who were willing to grow up enough to surrender any ideas that would prevent them from making their own laws, doing their own thing, and achieving self-sufficient power. That is how to be an "authentic person." What can the believer say in answer?

An Answer

To begin with, realize that the self-sufficient approach is neither new nor novel, let alone true. It is as old as the Book of Genesis. This position is almost a carbon copy of Genesis 3:1–8:

> Now the serpent was more crafty thàn any beast of the field which the LORD God had made. And he said to the woman, "Indeed, has God said, 'You shall not eat from any tree of the garden'?" The woman said to the serpent, "From the fruit of the trees of the garden we may eat; but from the fruit of the tree which is in the middle of the garden, God has said, 'You shall not eat from it or touch it, or you will die.'" The serpent said to

the woman, "You surely will not die! For God knows that in the day you eat from it your eyes will be opened, and you will be like God, knowing good and evil." When the woman saw that the tree was good for food, and that it was a delight to the eyes, and that the tree was desirable to make one wise, she took from its fruit and ate; and she gave also to her husband with her, and he ate. Then the eyes of both of them were opened, and they knew that they were naked; and they sewed fig leaves together and made themselves loin coverings.

They heard the sound of the Lord God walking in the garden in the cool of the day, and the man and his wife hid themselves from the presence of the Lord God among the trees of the garden.

The first truth found in Eden is that evil often comes camouflaged in a most subtle way. The serpent is a crafty, conniving, convincing con artist. He begins his conversation by carefully planting seeds of doubt: "Has God really said . . . ?"

Why do people seem so susceptible to such deception? The fact is we all are more readily deceived than we would like to admit. To go it alone and try to become as God, as did Adam and Eve, is unbelievably attractive. We love to be self-sufficient, to play God; but the result is self-deception. We believers, in attempting to share the truth of Christ with the postmodern of this ilk, should point out that people love the self-deception that says they can become self-sufficient and find God in their own self-oriented way. Slick half-truths are often worse than outright lies.

The second truth in Genesis, already implied, is the simple observable fact that whatever God forbids always seems most intriguing. Jesus described this phenomenon in his parable of the prodigal son (Luke 15:11–24). The young man felt he had come of age; he had to do his own thing. After all, he was self-sufficient. So the prodigal moved out to break the bonds of restrictions; off he went to conquer the world, only to end up in a pigpen, not as a free man but as an enslaved animal.

A life of independence from Jesus Christ always ends up in some sort of pigpen. An honest, objective look at life shows self-sufficiency to be a lie. Tell the postmoderns to look around, to look at their own selves. The human self alone never produces a full, rich, meaningful life. Help them face reality. It is not a pleasant picture, but they need to understand the truth spoken in love (Eph. 4:15).

It must be granted that from the very beginning God gave mankind the privilege of ruling creation. We are told to rule the world, but if we are going to govern our world as mature, authentic persons, we must first learn to govern ourselves. And that is only possible through faith in Christ. The self-discipline of faith constitutes the only key to "growing up." We simply cannot do it on our own. No one can. To think we can is not self-sufficiency; it is self-deception. It takes "God with us" to accomplish true, free selfhood. And God is not dead. He gave us objective laws of life designed to keep us from hurting ourselves. And, moreover, he imparts strength to do his will. That is where real life is found. When the Israelites ignored God and his commandments, when they did their own thing, they deteriorated into weakness and divisions. As a result, they were conquered and enslaved. All history verifies this reality for any people.

Christ and his way alone leads to genuine freedom. That is why the message of Christ is called *Good News*. That message enables us to grow into true selves. Stress this; it is an objective, absolute fact. Nietzsche stands as a classic case of the antithesis; he ended up insane. That tragic end may not occur for every person who turns away from God, but self-sufficiency is a road to emptiness if not destruction.

In Christ alone can we find true fulfillment, because he will be there to provide guidance, comfort, help, strength, and forgiveness when we need it, which is all the time, for we are dependent creatures and not supermen. "In Him we live and move and exist" (Acts 17:28). Yet that utter dependence is such that it does not destroy our freedom and responsibility. The point is one does not have to reject God to be free and responsible. To the contrary, real spirituality and freedom, which the postmoderns say they want, can be found only in a free, responsible commitment to Jesus Christ. All history and contemporary observation attest to these wonderful facts, as we shall see later in this chapter. Help the postmodern recognize this reality. It may knock down the straw man of self-seeking sufficiency that stands in the way of a clear hearing and heeding of the gospel.

The Bondage of Sin and Guilt

What does the postmodern do with sin and guilt? All people, at least to some extent, sense their guilt. They may strive to suppress it, but like the hound of hell, it never stops barking at their heels. "All have sinned" (Rom. 3:23). They may smirk at the idea, but their very reaction betrays their sense of guilt. Raise the question: Where do we find freedom from such guilt and frustration? No one will ever find freedom from guilt, emptiness, and futility except through Jesus Christ. For those who become Christians, the past is dead and buried with all its guilt and frustrations. Once we repent of our sin and accept Jesus Christ by faith, we are forgiven of everything. We truly are born again. We become a new creation (2 Cor. 5:17).

Freedom from Fear

Where does the postmodern find freedom from fear? Only Christian believers possess true freedom from frustration and anxiety. An Atlanta, Georgia, television station scored a victory in its ratings war with competing stations when it broadcast a series of reports on fear. They honed in on a subject that touches us all. Everyone suffers from fear of one sort or another. We are frightened to think about life's eventualities— of becoming crippled or losing those we love or a thousand other possibilities. A million potential disasters haunt us. But Christians who follow Christ know that he stands with us, waiting to help us in our struggles. He welcomes us into a totally new dimension of existence. If we keep our eyes on Jesus, we can walk without sinking amid the fearful storms of life. To be thick-skinned and say we have no fear is simply a retreat from reality. Nietzsche was simply self-deceived. No one is that strong, Nietzsche or anyone else. We are dependent creatures, like it or not. Therefore, can a truthful skeptic honestly address his or her own future without a subtle dread, born of a sense of nihilism? Can such people really fully convince themselves that they will not have to answer to God? It is doubtful. But there is help. The Word of God states, "For God hath not given us the spirit of fear, but of power, and of love, and of a sound mind" (2 Tim. 1:7 KJV). What a powerful truth to internalize and live and share!

Strength in Weakness

Where does the postmodern find freedom from overpowering temptations? Sin is always "crouching at the door" (Gen. 4:7). Guilt over the past and fear of the future can easily enslave us, but the greatest threat to our life is the temptation of the moment. In the deepest recesses of the hearts of all people, including the postmodern, rests the desire for forgiveness and peace with God. For those who know him, Christ grants victory and the joy of full forgiveness. Point this out clearly. We are not sufficient in ourselves to achieve peace; only Christ can do that.

Life in Christ can be summed up in Jesus' words: "If the Son sets you free, you will be free indeed" (John 8:36 NIV). Jesus Christ alone gives true freedom and genuine personhood. Inner freedom and peace do not rest in human self-sufficiency, which grows out of self-deception, if not satanic blindness. True selfhood comes in surrender to God. Our Lord said, "For whoever wishes to save his life will lose it, but whoever loses his life for My sake and the gospel's will save it" (Mark 8:35).

Of course, becoming a Christian does not ensure perfection. Believers still have struggles and sins. All of us have a long way to go; that we must grant. But true believers are traveling in the right direction. In

Christ one becomes an authentic self. Help the postmodern to see this. It may lead him or her to Christ.

"Religious" Atheist

In the postmodern desire for spirituality, there are few outright, propositional atheists, at least in the Nietzsche sense of the word. And even these at times appear rather "religious." As Paul said, they are "holding to a form of godliness, although they have denied its power" (2 Tim. 3:5). Then there are occasions when one does encounter an outright atheist. Some people have had a very negative experience, and "God did not help me," they say, so they turn away and deny him. Regardless of the depth of their atheistic views, "religious" or otherwise, we must discover what brought them to this point of denial. Usually it centers in the fact that they have had no experience of God at all, at least consciously. And, because of an existential approach to life and reality, they seriously question, or reject, the very existence of God. What can we say to these more extreme cases? Again, let it be stressed that we must always be sympathetic to honest doubters, as strange as their questions may seem to us who believe. Further, we all at times have our own problems, and thus we should see ourselves as fellow strugglers. But still we must have a word for those who have not experienced God, at least as it would seem on the surface.

An Answer

The argument begins by taking seriously and suggesting seriously the objective biblical invitation, "O taste and see that the LORD is good" (Ps. 34:8). God invites all people to take the faith test, to conduct a spiritual experiment and find out for themselves if he really is alive. He promises that those who seek him will find him: "You will find Him if you search for Him with all your heart" (Deut. 4:29). God really means it. If we truly seek God wholeheartedly, the experiment will not fail, even if we have doubts or question his reality.

There are sound reasons for accepting the invitation and seeing for oneself whether or not God exists. First, there is the subtle but very real universal spiritual hunger for God. Second, the testimony of others concerning the reality of God stands out in bold relief. Third, there is the lack of well-being for many that seems to have no answer in contemporary society. In all three areas there is testimony to the reality and existence of God. Even though we all struggle, there is a God who responds to our seeking. Let's look at these three truths in more depth. Actually, these realities have an application to all brands of postmodern unbelievers.

Spiritual Hunger

Psalm 42:1–2 describes humanity's deep-rooted hunger to know God: "My soul pants for You, O God. My soul thirsts for God, for the living God." As we have discovered, we are all creatures who want to know our Creator, as children desire to know their parents. Whether a person will acknowledge it or not, we are religious beings seeking answers to problems that only God in Christ can provide. For example, we desire goodness, but the best of us have some of the worst in us: "All have sinned, and come short of the glory of God" (Rom. 3:23 KJV). Even the crass skeptic, who denies the reality of sin, commits it and experiences guilt. How then do we find forgiveness for our sins and power to overcome future temptations? Only God through Jesus Christ can resolve that universal problem. Hence, the innate desire to know him personally is always there, subtle as it may be. As Augustine put it, "We are restless until we rest in Thee."

We all are aware of our need to love and be loved. But how often have people found a love that can outshine the darkness of hate? Is there a love that never grows old and cold? There is; God is love. To know him in his love is life's greatest goal. There is a vast difference between *eros* love (human love) and *agape* love (God's quality of love). And we all inwardly sense that and hence crave him, whether we realize it or not.

The glad and hearty affirmation of victory over all these and a thousand more pressing human needs is Jesus Christ, the ultimate answer to the human dilemma. Even the most skeptical must admit that Jesus has a wonderful magnetic appeal. An open-minded Hindu put it well: "There is no one else seriously bidding for the heart of the world except Jesus Christ."[13] There is something in us all that draws us to Jesus. The point is, Jesus by his Spirit stimulates the spiritual inclination of the sincere seeker (John 16:7–11). We believers can rightly assume that and build our witness on it, for this spiritual inclination is in everyone, even in personalities like the well-known existentialist and atheist Jean-Paul Sartre. He confessed that he once had experienced the presence of God, but he chose to resist God, suppress the urge toward God, and thus become a full-fledged atheist.[14]

What a mistake to reject the seeking God when he reveals himself and to retreat into some form of atheism! God's appeal touches the innermost nerve of all. Yet the right to resist that appeal is our God-given privilege. We were created with freedom. Sartre exercised his freedom, opting to suppress rather than express his religious stirrings. It seems that many have chosen to suppress their innate inclination and hunger for God, thus preempting any openness to God as revealed in the historic Jesus. Remember, an atheist is an atheist by his or her own choosing, not by God's failure to speak to and seek the unbeliever.

The Testimony of Others

Philosophers Thomas Altizer and William Hamilton, following Sartre's line, not only apparently suppressed their own spiritual instincts as God revealed himself, they also rather summarily dismissed the testimony of others concerning the reality of God in their lives. Thus they developed the "God is dead" philosophy and writings. Such a course is certainly not wise. The testimony of countless millions through the ages clearly points to the reality of God. The psalmist, even in the midst of his enemies, is able to say, "This I know, that God is for me" (Ps. 56:9). At the end of his excruciating ordeal, Job was able to say, "I have heard of You by the hearing of the ear; but now my eye sees You" (Job 42:5). God is there right in the midst of life, in its joys and in its pain. Job had begun by believing God, but then he came to know him in a new, fresh, in-depth way. Can we accept the testimonies of the psalmist and Job? Yes, because they are reinforced by the fact that they and a multitude of others are trustworthy people.

A mere cursory survey of history clearly demonstrates that reliable people of every age and culture have had unmistakable, genuine experiences of God. What is particularly impressive centers in the fact that we have well-documented testimonies from intelligent, well-balanced, and believable individuals. Even Einstein believed in a supreme Being. How could so many be so wrong? This can often touch the atheist. True, the argument from religious experience does not incontestably prove God, but to ignore such a mountain of evidence is hardly honest investigation. It cannot be so easily set aside as the secularist or postmodern might have us believe.

Blaise Pascal was one of the world's greatest physicists and mathematicians. He became absolutely convinced that God was not only alive but also a living part of his life. He compared his encounter with God's Spirit to a fire. God's presence had warmed his heart, enlightened his mind, and set his conscience on fire. It is an inner revolution, testified Pascal. Is he not a reasonable witness for Christianity?

C. S. Lewis was perhaps the most astute twentieth-century defender of the faith. He was an atheist before being converted to Christ. His move toward a Christian conversion reached a critical point while he was riding a bus. He suddenly realized that he was suppressing spiritual realities and his inner hunger for God. He knew he had to make a choice whether or not to open his mind, heart, and life to the God who truly does confront people. As he faced that choice, he saw that his life was a "zoo of lusts, bedlam of ambition, a nursery of fears, and harem of fouled hates."[15]

Lewis turned to Jesus Christ with all his heart and discovered that God works wonders in yielded lives. C. S. Lewis, professor of English literature at Oxford and then Cambridge, went on to become a literary evangelist for Jesus Christ, proclaiming that anyone can find new life in Christ and know God in a deep and personal way if he or she will but yield to him. That is the issue; the seeker must be willing to yield to God as he or she seeks him wholeheartedly. Surrender finds the Savior. And in Lewis's words, one will be "surprised by joy."

Back in the turbulent 1960s, the years that gave impetus to much postmodernism, as the death of God theology was making news, Billy Graham was interviewed on the NBC morning news program *Today*. When asked how he knew God was not dead, Graham replied, "Because I spoke to him this morning." That is not a glib or shallow answer. Such a testimony is based on genuine religious experience. It can, of course, be rejected, but it cannot be refuted. One simply cannot prove Graham did not talk with God, and Graham is not alone. Millions of sensible, honest Christians know God is alive because they have "experienced" him. Testimonies are powerful. In the Book of Revelation we read, "They defeated him [Satan] by the blood of the Lamb, and by their testimony; for they did not love their lives but laid them down for him" (Rev. 12:11 TLB).

Social Well-Being

Remember Jesus' healing of the blind man? The religious leaders who were opposing the Lord tried to discredit the report of that healing, but the blind man did not falter under their cross-examination. He declared, "One thing I do know, that though I was blind, now I see" (John 9:25). Someone else has said:

> One thing we know: The most successful cure for alcoholism and every other drug addiction is a personal experience with Jesus Christ.
>
> One thing we know: The most successful defense against family disaster is having a home where people follow Christ.
>
> One thing we know: The most successful therapy for emotional troubles is rooted in a relationship with Christ.
>
> One thing we know: The most successful solution to social evils is a spiritual revival where people feel the full impact of God's love in their lives.

Who could come into a dynamic experience of Jesus Christ and fail to be a better person? Granted, there is much superficial Christianity today. There always has been and probably always will be. But surely a true experience with Christ changes life for the better. All society benefits from genuine Christian experience. Point the postmodern to these facts.

Some declare that we can create a better world if we are divorced from traditional, transcendental Christianity. That has been the basic argument of secular humanists of all stripes for hundreds of years and can be traced back to the tower of Babel. Are they right?

Harold J. Brown, professor of law at Harvard University Law School, states that separation from our traditional religious values has brought us to the point where "our whole culture seems to be facing the possibility of a nervous breakdown."[16] The skeptical postmodern should be reminded of that sad truth. And just to say, as they may, that they are not giving up the ethics or morals of Christianity will never do. No one can live out the ethics of Jesus without the transcendental experience of knowing Jesus personally in religious experience, because that is where the power to live out Christian morality is found. Moral precepts alone are not enough. They must be lived out in a person's life, and that can be done only through Jesus Christ.

Contemporary writers who have chosen to experience nothing but the absence of God have tended to produce novels and dramas that are preoccupied with violence, immorality, perversion, and self-destructiveness. There are few real heroes—healthy and happy characters. There are exceptions, of course, but the general rule holds. Dismissing God in Christ is always ultimately destructive, despite any claim to hold on to morals and spirituality. Society today testifies to this reality. Even atheistic philosopher Thomas Altizer admitted that the God-less life could possibly lead to "madness and dehumanization" and "moral chaos and life destroying nihilism."[17] If that is possible, even remotely as Altizer admits, it seems a total mystery why anyone would want to embrace such a stand and reject Christ. Truth always produces good, not evil. That basic logic is somehow overlooked or ignored or forgotten in many lives today. Look at contemporary society. The postmodern worldview simply does not work, socially or individually.

Such truths should convince anyone to conduct the spiritual experiment of faith. Take the faith test and see how good the Good News actually is. With the living Christ, there is hope for a better world and life. Without the Lord, what is left? "In Him all things hold together" (Col. 1:17). Not only the postmoderns, but the old-line moderns need to realize this. There stands an argument for them to ponder.

Questions and Issues for Study

1. What is the root cause for doubts about the Christian faith?
2. What various avenues do these doubts take and why?
3. Why are believers at times so inept at giving an answer to doubters?
4. Can the Christian faith be rightly defended?
5. What must one do to be a good apologist?
6. What spirit must the apologist have to be convincing to the doubter?
7. Do apologetics alone convert doubters?
8. What defenses can be made to various aspects of postmodern doubts?
9. Do people really seek God?
10. What is the final answer all people must hear?

four

Constructing a Christian Worldview for Postmoderns and Moderns Alike

What about the "moderns" still among us? Do we have answers for their skepticism as well as for that of postmoderns? The answer is a resounding yes. But first, every endeavor in developing a worldview demands a starting point. All must be helped to realize this fact, and this does not leave out the postmoderns or moderns. Moreover, how one starts largely determines direction and thus where one ultimately arrives. Constructing a Christian worldview proves to be no exception. Therefore, the question that thrusts itself to the fore is, How and where does one begin?

In answer to the above foundational query, Professor Clark Pinnock said the following:

> The central problem for theology is *its own epistemological base*. From what fountainhead does theology acquire the information from which she forms

her doctrinal models and tests her hypotheses? What is the *principium the-ologia,* which measures and authenticates the subject matter for theology and preaching? No endeavor in theology can *begin* until some kind of answer is given. . . . All issues pale before this one. It is the continental divide in Christian theology. Everything hangs on our solution to it.[1]

Professor Pinnock is certainly correct in saying that the issue of finding authority for theological truth claims, as it emerges out of a comprehensive epistemological base, stands as the primary issue in fabricating a proper worldview. The key question is, How does a person authenticate what he or she says about God's truth and reality? That constitutes the starting point.

Constructing an epistemological base whereby one can form "doctrinal models and test . . . hypotheses," as Pinnock put it, is an individual's initial responsibility. The venture into the ambiguous world of epistemology is not pursued without some fear and perhaps presumption. It is fearful because first of all it may call for a measure of rather plodding, pedantic argumentation. Then, second, it is an attempt to discover authoritative truth. That may be somewhat presumptuous, for such truth is in some respects quite difficult to uncover. However, fearful and presumptuous, or not, we must forge ahead, for Pinnock was absolutely right: "No endeavor in theology can *begin*" until this is accomplished.

The Epistemological Base for Christian Faith Claims

Epistemology can be defined as the branch of philosophy that investigates the origin, structure, methods, and validity of knowledge. The term *theory of knowledge* is a common English equivalent of epistemology. In simple terms, epistemology essentially seeks to discover the sources of reliable and authoritative truth and the way one thus comes into contact with reality. Everyone operates with some sort of epistemology. Everyone resorts to some basis of authority for his or her truth claims. Thus everyone does have an epistemology and needs to be aware of his or her epistemological methodologies, especially we believers in our claims concerning God and the need of Jesus Christ in our life. The apologetic spin-off is obvious.

The task of building an explicit epistemological base for an individual can be launched by examining the interplay of the mind with reality as a person comes into contact with what he or she conceives to be sources of truth, that is, those "mechanisms" whereby the person thinks he or she comes into contact with truth and reality. Actually, there are several such "sources" to which the mind reacts.

Empirical Data

The first obvious source of contact with truth is through what philosophers call *empiricism*, that is, sense perception. Everyone comes into regular encounters with the real world through sense perception. For example, as I write these words, I feel the pen in my hand, see the words appearing on the page, and hear the subtle scratch of the pen point on paper. What a person sees, touches, smells, tastes, and hears enables him or her to become aware of the "facts" of the world out there and constitutes an empirical experience. Those facts are called empirical data, perceived by the mind's empirical faculties. Normally a person relies on those empirical mechanisms to make what is considered to be truth claims about the real world. Hence, an individual daily makes statements like: "I was there; I saw it; I know it is true." Much of human awareness of the objective world comes through empirical data. Philosopher William Barkley went so far as to say that "to be is to be perceived."

Rational Concepts

Another clear claim to truth is *rationalism*. This epistemological principle gets a hefty workout every day. For example, whenever two plus two is added correctly, the conclusion has been reached through the rationalistic, logical process. All mathematical reasoning is an extension of rational logic, even the complex labyrinths of higher mathematics, such as Einstein's $E=MC^2$. Another example of logical rationalism is the simple Aristotelian syllogism: All people are mortal. I am a person. Therefore, I am mortal.

Everyone uses this epistemological principle constantly, being quite confident that statements like "two plus two equals five" stand in error, because they fail the rational criteria of truth. We regularly bring such rational tests to life's encounters to validate what claims to be true. Remember, this was Hegel's beginning—and ending—line.

A Priori Truth

Then there is a little more obscure principle called a priori truth. A priori concepts are those innate realities we find "just there." One cannot rationally or empirically demonstrate them, at least not incontestably. Still, we sense they are there and are real. What are some of these a priori realities? A big debate rages as to whether they exist at all, let alone what they are. But most thinkers positive to the general idea list things like *self-consciousness* (René Descartes held to this), *moral consciousness* (Immanuel Kant argued for this, calling it the "categorical imperative"), and *the concept of God* (many able thinkers hold to this position). We assume these truths as part of our cognitive (thinking) activities because, when we think, we discover them simply *there*. I find it rather difficult even to think without granting at least some a priori realities. Descartes had it right when he said, "I think, therefore I am." I assume my own self-consciousness when I think. Can anyone *really* think about *all* reality and deny there are at least some a priori principles? Too many vistas of truth and reality are barred from investigation if one refuses to accept the validity of a priori concepts, even if they are relatively few in number.

There may well be other epistemological principles (sources from which we discover truth and reality), such as *intuitionism*. Intuitionism is the innate sense that something is true even if it does not lend itself to purely empirical, rational verification. Nonetheless, the above principles illustrate some general precepts of epistemology.

Revelational Truth

There is another epistemological principle that Christians put forth as a source of truth. Believers in Jesus Christ hold to the epistemological principle called *revelation* and place great importance on it. Christians declare God has revealed himself, and from such a self-disclosure, we can arrive at authoritative truth concerning God's nature, actions, and expectations, and the final reason for many sorts of phenomenon. This is an epistemological truth claim believers continually make. However, this principle seems to raise questions.

"Oh," retorts the modern—and postmodern—critic concerning revelational truth claims, "One must have *faith* to accept as true the concepts Christians claim God *reveals* about himself. One must *believe* to say any revelation is true." The clear implication of this quite common rejoinder to the Christian witness is that empiricism, rationalism, and a priori concepts are on a different plane of authority than revelation, because a person has to *believe* to accept revelational realities. They seem to say (at least the more unsophisticated thinkers) that empiricism and rationalism need no faith to be accepted as valid sources of truth. They imply, and may well believe, their epistemological principles stand superior to revelation, because they feel they need no faith to authenticate them. Are they right? If they are, believers do have a problem, for revelational truth claims certainly are faith-demanding presuppositions.

An Important Principle

Here arises a most important fact: *All epistemological principles are what philosophers call presuppositions.* In other words, they are all assumptions on which one operates in cognition. Very few, if any, epistemologists deny this central reality. Empiricism, rationalism, a priori concepts, and intuitionism, as well as revelation, all involve a presuppositional stance. Their validity cannot be demonstrated incontestably; hence, they are *presupposed* as valid sources of truth and reality.

Why can their validity not be incontestably established? The reason is quite obvious; one must assume these types of epistemological principles to use them. For example, we are forced to assume, or presuppose, the validity of empiricism to arrive at what we think is true from empirical input. We are compelled to believe that empiricism is a valid source of truth about reality to accept empirical data when it is encountered. Simply put, one has to assume and use empiricism to "prove" empirical data. So we must *believe* our sense perception is bringing us in contact with reality. Thus it is a presupposition. In that light, all such epistemological principles are presuppositions.

The conclusion to this epistemological principle jumps right out at us. In light of the fact that all epistemological sources of truth are presuppositional in nature, it takes faith or believing to accept and assimilate any epistemological truth claims. All presuppositions are a "leap of faith." Therefore, empiricism, rationalism, a priori concepts, and intuitionism rest on the same epistemological "leap of faith" plane as does revelation. They all demand believing in that cognitive sense. So revelation, at least in principle, stands as a valid claim to truth as much as any other epistemological claim. Revelational truth claims just cannot be a priori ruled out of court by implying they rest on another epistemological level because it takes a leap of faith to accept it. All truth claims rest on that same plane in principle.

Valid Source of Truth

Probably the reason revelation seems different to many is the fact that we live much of our daily life thinking about empirical and rational realities. Familiarity with these sorts of truth claims elevates them in our thinking above the claims of revelation. Moreover, the Western world's virtual worship of the scientific method, which is a purely rational-empirical methodology, has no doubt deepened the problem as well. Even infatuation with materialism has contributed to this attitude. But again let it be stressed that all the epistemological principles we have been discussing are presuppositions, demanding faith to accept their claims, and thus, in principle, are established on the same basis.

Therefore, Christian believers need not take a backseat regarding revelational truth claims and feel they cannot prove their claims as can the materialistic skeptics with their empirical-rational methodologies. They cannot prove their claims, either. In a very real sense, all truth claims, because they are presuppositions, defy final, formal, utterly incontestable proof of reality. This may sound as if we do not really know anything for certain. I suppose, in a formal sense, we do not. But such is hardly a tenable, workable epistemology. All people live and act on what they believe to be true. So may it be stressed, revelation is, in principle, as valid a source of truth as anything else, at least in the formal fashion we have been arguing.

Actually, a solid case can be made for accepting a revelational presupposition because revelation provides data to develop a far more comprehensive, broader understanding of reality than we would otherwise have. It opens up realms of truth and reality that are unavailable through other data. The mature Christian believer is not actually a narrow-minded thinker as often accused; he or she is broader in epistemological scope because of the acceptance of another source of truth and reality—revelation. That presuppositional acceptance can display beautiful vistas of reality otherwise barred from one's cognitive life.

The more of reality one accepts, the more valid it makes one's worldview. The scientists and others who restrict themselves to empirical and rationalistic presuppositions alone are actually the narrow-minded people. Of course they can reject revelation as a source of truth; such is their cognitive privilege. However, that is probably why the scientific method in isolation fails to explain *all* reality. A purely rational-empirical epistemology simply cannot explain spiritual realities, not even realities like love or peace of mind, let alone God. Utopia, as is now clear, is not to be found in the laboratory. That is one of the reasons postmodernism arose. So revelational presuppositions are not only as valid as others in principle, but also they help create a more comprehensive, coherent worldview.

An Epistemological Game

Everyday life is obviously filled with the cognitive, presuppositional exercise we have been discussing. That is how we arrive at what we consider true and real, and in such a cognitive setting we constantly play a little game.

When we were children, many of us played the game we called "king of the hill." Remember how it went? You would climb to the top of a small hill, then your playmates would scramble up in an attempt to send you tumbling down so they might take their stand on the top as king of the hill.

Epistemologically, we constantly play that sort of game. At one time we make empiricism king, at other times rationalism. That is, on one occasion we rely primarily on our empirical experience to give us truth; on other occasions rationalism takes first place. There is some balance between the competing players of course. But this cognitive exercise is how we attempt to arrive at a coherent view of reality.

Persons normally play the cognitive game quite unconsciously. But if a conscious conflict between two or more epistemological presuppositions arises, the balance breaks, and then the game becomes very explicit, if not quite disturbing. For example, seeing a cow flying by the window causes a real cognitive dilemma. Rationally, people know cows do not fly, but we just saw one sail by. Suddenly rationalism and empiricism come into conflict with each other. So persons have to play king of the hill to decide which presupposition—the rational or the empirical—is going to be king. Which will get top priority, or authority, rational awareness or empirical experience? A decision must be made to resolve the cognitive dilemma. Did experience show a cow flying or not? This illustration is an extreme instance, but people play the game constantly.

Whenever or however an epistemological conflict arises, people try desperately to work out the solution because we all demand that the world of cognitive experiences be internally *coherent*. The world must hold together and make sense on the basis of epistemological experiences. Human beings cannot live with major epistemological conflicts raging. Coherence is the constant quest of the mind, and those who cease to demand coherence in their thinking processes become psychotic. Thus people play the king-of-the-hill game and decide which epistemological presupposition will rise as the top authority in given situations. This process resolves most dilemmas, even if a mystery is left on rare occasions.

The Final Authority

How does all of this relate to Christian commitment to truth derived from revelation, which is, as we have seen, as valid a presupposition as rationalism or any of the other epistemological presuppositions? What do people do with revelational presupposition as they cognitively build their system of truth, especially Christian truth? Simply put, how does revelation stand relative to other epistemological presuppositions? Well, if there is no conflict between revelation and, for example, rationalism, no problem is raised. As a case of point, when the Bible (which evangelical Christians hold is revelational truth) says that Jesus sat by the Sea of Galilee and taught, there is no rational or empirical conflict with revelation. Someone sitting by a seaside and teaching is not irrational or nonempirical. There should be no problem on such issues. However, when Jesus walked across the water to the other side of the sea, that is a rational problem. Rationally, no one walks on water. We have a serious conflict between rationalism and revelation. What do we do? There is no alternative; we must play king of the hill. Which epistemological presupposition will get our vote for final truth and authority? Will we accept the revelational claim that Jesus walked on the water, or will we settle for rationalism and say the Bible is in error? A decision must be made for our world to be coherent.

Evangelical Christians and the wise witness for Christ have opted for revelation as the *final* authority for truth and reality when such cognitive conflicts arise. They make revelation king of the hill. Evangelicals do not deny rationalism and empirical claims when there is no conflict; they simply place revelation as superior when and if a real conflict between competing principles surfaces. Obviously all thinkers, even some who profess Christianity, do not take this position. There are those who, when it comes to the crunch, put their stock in rationalism or intuitionism or some other presuppositional approach. Consequently they develop some explanation for subjugating an obvious revelational claim to another epistemological presupposition, for they too must have a coherent world to keep their own sanity. We cannot just ignore a competing claim. But evangelicals traditionally choose revelation as the theological king of presuppositions.

The Primary Issue

Is it wise for evangelicals to hold that revelation is the proper king of the hill when epistemological presuppositions come in conflict with revelational claims? Perhaps the answer is found in a prior question: *Does this approach of most evangelicals produce the most comprehensive worldview?* Is the evangelical-revelational epistemology, as over against a pure rational-empirical approach, theologically or otherwise the most comprehensive view of reality? Is it internally coherent, does it correspond to the experience of reality, is it noncontradictory, and does it best encompass and explain our apprehension of truth and reality? The most comprehensive, noncontradicting, corresponding, coherent view is obvi-

ously the best view. Thus evangelicals are forced to bring to their reve-
lational-superiority claims the test of things fitting together in a system
that makes the best sense of life and reality. If they are to make those
claims stick, they must show that a revelational epistemology really does
pass the test with the highest marks. Can it be done? The conviction of
evangelical thinkers is yes; revelational supremacy in truth claims concerning God and reality does produce the best, inclusive epistemological approach to truth and reality. They hold it passes the tests of inter-
nal coherence, noncontradiction, and correspondence with the highest
marks. It corresponds to reality more comprehensively than any other
approach.

I confess I take my epistemological stand with evangelicals on the
supremacy of revelation in truth about God and the world. But can one
argue convincingly for such an epistemological cause? Again the answer
is yes, because it makes life more fulfilling and meaningful and answers
questions that can be answered in no other way. It is thus wise to accept
the revelational claims of the Holy Scriptures, which answer the deepest questions of life and thus make the most sense of it.

Moreover, J. S. Stewart, New Testament scholar, points out that the
wise person will recognize in Jesus Christ all he claims to be—the Son
of Man and Son of God. In Stewart's book *The Strong Name*, he demonstrates that Jesus does have a claim on every person because of:

- The mystery of his *personality*. All history tells us he was a capti-
  vating personality. He was truly human.
- The mystery of his *power*. Through Jesus' influence for two thousand years, great positive events have taken place. He is truly God.
- The mystery of his *presence*. He does speak and reveal himself to
  people unmistakably, if they will but listen to him for all he is.
- All of this leads to recognizing Christ's sinlessness, his divine abilities, his universal appeal, and the peace of conscience he gives in
  forgiveness.[2]

The person of Jesus Christ is a "mystery" unless one takes him for all he
is—fully *God* and fully *Man* who died and rose again for our sins. The
Lord Jesus convinces people of his personality, power, presence, and
the source of a whole new life if they will but give him a hearing. That
is what really makes sense of life. It answers life's deepest questions
most fully. The wise witness makes that clear after the argument from
epistemology is made. And that is sound from any epistemological worldview perspective. Revelation makes sense. Jesus gives life at its best.

Conclusion

Thus we are back to the root of Christianity—Jesus Christ. He is alive. He fulfills the innate longing for God. The testimony of the ages is valid. He makes the difference between chaos and a viable life and society. He lives and will reveal himself to the true seeker. He gives a whole new, meaningful life to those who believe. Christianity is simply the best worldview. That fact is vital to understand—and to communicate to doubting moderns and postmoderns. To put it simply: to become a Christian really makes sense out of life. Jesus Christ himself becomes our worldview.

Thus a twofold responsibility rests on the church. First, the church needs to be led to engage moderns and postmoderns of contemporary society. We must be moved out of our comfort zone and engage people without Christ as we find them. Remember, the church is a witnessing community. Second, the church must be equipped to meet all in society with its radically different worldview. This chapter and the preceding one are only a beginning on how contemporary Christians need to be trained and taught in apologetics and in gospel presentation. We have a new challenge as God's people. It is my hope that the rest of this book will help us rise to the occasion and create an effective evangelistic church.

A Summary of Apologetic Principles for Postmoderns

- When speaking to postmoderns we must speak in a language and use words they will understand from their cultural background. If we must use a theological or biblical term they may not grasp, we should define and explain it. This is a necessary communication principle.
- In their quest for spirituality, we can help them see that a vague quest without definite convictions concerning the personhood of God will never satisfy. In a word, they need Jesus Christ, and that constitutes an absolute truth.
- They must realize that God has revealed himself, and because of who God is he *must* reveal himself if we are to know him at all. We can lead them to see that God has revealed himself in Christ, and that is sensible.
- In their denial of absolutes, we should lead them to recognize that absolutes are all around us every day. Even to say there are no absolutes is an absolute statement. If we encounter absolutes in the more mundane things of life, how much more must it be true

of things that matter most, such as God, morality, truth, and so on. It makes real cognitive sense to believe God and receive Christ as Lord and Savior.

- Help the postmodern recognize that his or her rejection of materialism does not save him or her from humanism. A simple, self-centered life is the epitome of humanism.
- Lead postmoderns to recognize that mere psychological contentment is a far cry from the peace God gives in Christ.
- Point out that a real, logical case can be made for God's revelation in Christ. He is the final answer to a meaningful worldview.
- Finally, point out to the postmodern the reality of sin, judgment, and hell. These are unavoidable, inescapable realities. Share the ultimate remedy for all human problems—forgiveness and salvation that rest in the Lord Jesus Christ. *Present the full gospel.* All apologetics finally must lead to this. Rely on the Holy Spirit to give you words and break down barriers. Then share the Savior. And remember, the gospel truly is "the power of God for salvation" (Rom. 1:16). The church can share it with confidence.

In this context we share the message of Christ. But what is that message? To this central concern we turn next.

Questions and Issues for Study

1. What do you understand *apologetics* to mean?
2. Why are apologetics important for postmoderns?
3. What line do you think is best to take with postmoderns?
4. What role does a meaningful relationship with postmoderns play?
5. How do you help people see that "spirituality" is not enough?
6. How do you knock down the barriers that keep them from an openness to Christ?
7. How does one deal with the exclusiveness of Jesus Christ?
8. What is the role of the different apologetic approaches?
9. What do you see as the best apologetic today?
10. How do you get the gospel in during your conversations with postmoderns?

five

The Proclamation
of the Good News of God

At this stage of our investigating the New Age and how to reach its members for Christ, it must be stated again that, regardless of the postmodern worldview and apologetic efforts needed to overcome the barriers it raises, there must never be any compromise concerning the gospel of Jesus Christ. The *kerygma* (proclamation) in its biblical entirety must be shared with all. An effectual apologetic in that context is important, but first let the church understand and learn the full nature of our message of Christ.

What then is the church's message? What is that "foolishness" of the proclamation (1 Cor. 1:21) that God uses to save people? The implication of Paul's statement to the Corinthians constitutes a vitally important issue in regard to effectual evangelistic communication. It deserves a close investigation. Bible scholars have for many years given much guidance in this vital area of evangelization. This chapter stresses the preacher's role, but the principles apply to teaching, personal witnessing, or any other communication of Christ's message.

Approaches to the *Kerygma*

C. H. Dodd

Ever since professor C. H. Dodd gave us his classic little volume *The Apostolic Preaching and Its Development,* keen interest has centered on the idea conveyed by the New Testament word *kerygma.* Paul said in 1 Corinthians 1:21, "For since in the wisdom of God the world through its wisdom did not come to know God, God was well-pleased through the foolishness of the message preached *[kerygma]* to save those who believe." This passage makes the importance of the *kerygma* patent, for in the term we find the essence of the Good News the church is to proclaim in all evangelistic endeavors.

As Dodd approaches the subject, he first makes a quite unbending distinction between two Greek terms, *kerygma* and *didaskein. Didaskein* the professor defines as teaching, i.e., ethical and moral instructions on the Christian life. Occasionally, he tells us, it includes what we today call apologetics. And as has been stressed, that is important for the postmodern. At other times *didaskein* contains theological doctrine, for example, in the Johannine writing. But *didaskein* is quite distinct from *kerygma. Kerygma* is preaching, preaching of the nature of a "public proclamation of Christianity to the non-Christian world."[1] Through the proclamation of the kerygmatic gospel, the church evangelized its contemporary culture. Dodd fears that much of the preaching in the church today might not have been recognized by the early Christians as kerygma. What is heard in large measure on Sunday morning in many congregations is either teaching, exhortation *(paraklusis),* or a *homilia,* a discussion on the Christian life and thought directed toward those who already believe. Evangelistic preaching in the New Testament sense of the word, Dodd contends, has for its object—at least the great bulk of the time—the full gospel of Jesus Christ. He holds that the basic idea contained in the term *kerygssein* is so close to that conveyed by the word *evangelizesthai* (to evangelize) that for all practical purposes the terms can be used synonymously.[2] He deduces:

> For the early church, then, to preach the Gospel was by no means the same thing as to deliver moral instruction or exhortation. While the church was concerned to hand on the teaching of the Lord, it was not by this that it made converts. It was by *kerygma,* says Paul, not by *didache,* that it pleased God to save men.[3]

What then is this primitive *kerygma,* as Dodd sees it? What constitutes the essence of the Christian message with conversion as the goal?

In the preaching of Peter and others, as found in early Acts, Dodd discerns six basic elements in their *kerygma*. First, the age of fulfillment has dawned. The messianic age has arrived (Acts 2:16–21). Second, this new age has taken place through the ministry, death, and resurrection of Jesus Christ. And a brief account of this is *always* given (Acts 2:22–24). The concepts of the Davidic descent, the Lord's ministry, his vicarious death, and his glorious resurrection are invariably presented. Moreover, these truths are presented in the context of scriptural prophecy fulfilled, as determined by the foreknowledge of God. Third, by virtue of the resurrection, our Lord has been elevated to the right hand of God as messianic head of the "new Israel" (Acts 2:33–36). Fourth, the Holy Spirit is given as the sign of Christ's present power and glory (Acts 2:33). Fifth, the messianic age will reach its consummation at the return of Christ (Acts 3:21). And lastly, the *kerygma* in Acts closes with an appeal for repentance, the offer of forgiveness, the gift of the Holy Spirit, and the assurance of salvation in the life of the "age to come" (Acts 2:38–39). Dodd then summarizes, "We may take it that this is what the author of Acts meant by 'preaching the kingdom of God.' "[4]

Dodd's understanding of the essential *kerygma* in Paul's epistles can be summarized as follows:

> The prophecies are fulfilled and the new age is inaugurated by the coming of Jesus Christ, God's Son.
>
> He was born of the seed of David.
>
> He died according to the Scriptures to deliver us out of the present evil age.
>
> He was buried.
>
> He rose on the third day according to the Scriptures.
>
> He is exalted at the right hand of God, as Son of God and Lord of the living and dead.
>
> He will come again as Judge and Savior of men.

Dodd grants that the evangelistic preaching of Paul probably contained more than this, but it includes at least the elements listed above for it to be called evangelistic proclamation at all.

Professor Dodd condenses it well in his commentary on 1, 2, and 3 John. He writes:

> The crisis of history has arrived; the prophecies are fulfilled; and the "Age to Come" has begun.
>
> Jesus of Nazareth, of the line of David, came as God's Son, the Messiah.

He did mighty works; gave a new and authoritative teaching or law; was crucified, dead and buried (died for our sins); rose again the third day; was exalted to "the right hand of God," victorious over "principalities and powers"; will come again as Judge of quick and dead.

The apostles and those who are in fellowship with them constitute the Church, the New Israel of God, marked out as such by the outpouring of the Spirit.

Therefore repent, believe in Christ, and you will receive forgiveness of sins and a share in the life of the Age to Come (or eternal life).[5]

A contrast between the Pauline proclamation and the Jerusalem *kerygma* makes it clear that Paul emphasized three things that are not as explicit in the proclamation found in the early chapters of Acts. First of all, in early Acts Jesus is not normally called the "Son of God." His titles are more in line with the prophecies of Isaiah. But Dodd states that the idea of Jesus as Son of God is deeply embodied in the Synoptic Gospels, and these first three books of the New Testament were probably little influenced by Paul. The preachers of early Acts were surely not averse to the idea of Jesus as Son of God.

Second, the Jerusalem *kerygma,* as compared with Paul's preaching, says little about Christ's dying *for* our sins. As Dodd puts it, "the result of the life, death, and resurrection of Christ is the forgiveness of sins, but the forgiveness is not specifically connected with His death."[6]

Third, the Jerusalem *kerygma* does not emphatically assert that the ascended Lord intercedes for us, as does Paul. As for the rest of the points in Paul's gospel, they are all found in the early sermons of Acts.

The differences between Paul's preaching and that in early Acts surely do not imply any sort of contradiction. As New Testament writer George S. Duncan in his commentary on Galatians contends, there are not two gospels, the Jewish and Gentile.[7] The emphasis of Paul probably grew out of his days of meditation on the implications of the Christ event, particularly in the concept that Christ died as a substitute for our sins. In early Acts, the church hardly had time to put all the theological implications and conclusions of the Christ event together. Moreover, Paul was essentially addressing a Gentile world, not a Jewish one. The messianic concept would mean little to a Gentile, but Jesus as the Son of God would. The apostle was most wise to preach the Word in a fashion that would address the Gentile culture and mind-set. For example, at Athens Paul referred to their poets, not the Old Testament prophets, at least in the early stages of addressing the Athenian philosophers. This principle is what I am contending for in addressing postmoderns. We must "talk their language."

Michael Green

Since the time Dodd wrote his classic work on the *kerygma,* the book-shelves of believers and Christian leaders have been lined with volumes that build on his essential thesis. Criticisms of Dodd's approach have naturally arisen. For example, Michael Green, New Testament scholar and special envoy of the Archbishop of Canterbury for evangelism, has contended that in Dodd, "there has been undue concentration on what has become technically known as the *'kerygma.'* "[8] He holds that Dodd has made the *kerygma* far too "fixed." At one point he even raises the question as to whether or not there even was a fixed *kerygma.*[9] He argues that "the probabilities of the situation would militate against undue fixity in the presentation of the message."[10] What is to be grasped, Green argues, is that the background and understanding of the listeners significantly determined what aspect of the truth of Christ was to be declared. Green tells us:

It would be a mistake to assume from studies such as those of Dodd that there was a crippling uniformity about the proclamation of Christian truth in antiquity. That there was a basic homogeneity in what was preached we may agree, but there was wide variety in the way it was presented. Nor was this variety always the result of the supposedly rigid and conflicting theologies, which were prevalent in different sections of the ancient church. . . . But much of the variety will have been necessitated by the needs and understanding of the hearers. Evangelism is never proclamation in a vacuum; but always to people, and the message must be given in terms that make sense to them.[11]

Green is not alone in this contention. This is also the approach of Professor C. F. D. Moule in his book *The Birth of the New Testament.* Edward Schweizer writes along similar lines in an essay found in *Current Issues in New Testament Interpretation.* Perhaps the best full-scale treatment of this problem is found in R. C. Worley's work *Preaching and Teaching in the Early Church.*[12]

Still, Green grants, "there was a basic homogeneity in what was preached." He believes we shall not go far wrong in taking three basic points as essential to the evangelistic message that the first-century church proclaimed. First, they preached a person. Their message was frankly and unapologetically Christocentric. This gospel message was not so much centered on Christ's life and public ministry; rather, it rested on his death and glorious resurrection.

The second basic point of the message had to do with gifts—the gift of forgiveness, the gift of the Holy Spirit, the gift of adoption and reconciliation, with the emphasis on the gift of forgiveness and the gift of the Holy Spirit. These gifts of God's grace made "no people" the "people of God."

Third, the first-century church looked for a response from their hearers. The apostles were anything but shy in asking people to decide then and there for or against Christ. They expected results, positive results. These early preachers declared that people must do three things in response to the gospel:

1. They must repent. This was first and foremost.
2. They must exercise faith. A continuing life of faith was called for, but it must begin by a "leap of faith." True faith is inseparable from repentance.
3. They must be baptized. Baptism was seen as the seal on God's offer of forgiveness and as the essence of people's response to that offer in repentance and faith.[13]

From this perspective, Green presents his understanding of the *kerygma*. And though there may be some validity in his criticisms of Dodd's approach, it is certainly clear he also sees the essential proclamation as a definable, propositional body of theological truth. One wonders if he, in essence, has merely rearranged Dodd's propositions in a different fashion. Be that as it may, the listeners did influence the manner of presentation. The early preachers contextualized the gospel, and we must do the same today if we are to reach postmoderns. But we must always remember that the heart of the gospel *never* changes.

Douglas Webster

In something of the spirit of Michael Green, Douglas Webster in *Yes to Mission* presents his grasp of the *kerygma* in four basic principles. He begins by reminding readers that "mission implies that the Church does have something to say."[14] He states that evangelistic preaching must always center on:

1. The person and character of Jesus Christ. He really did live and was unique above all other men.
2. The teaching of Jesus Christ. He said things about God, life, the kingdom of God, and human destiny as no one had ever spoken before.
3. The death of Jesus Christ. The death of our Lord was the turning point in all history, and God was ultimately active in it.

4. The resurrection of Jesus Christ. Death did not end it all for the Lord; rather it was the end of death, for he is a living Savior.

Webster correctly points out that though some want to add more to the gospel than the above four essential points, it is certain that "we cannot have less, if we are to retain the Gospel at all."[15]

James Stewart

Another writer on the theme of proclamation is James Stewart in his insightful book *A Faith to Proclaim.* In this helpful volume he tells us that the first axiom of evangelism centers in the fact that the witness must be sure of the message. However, he does not, on his own admission, attempt to traverse again the ground that Dodd and others have covered in attempting to discover the primitive *kerygma.* His purpose is to find the bearing the *kerygma* has on present-day questions. This is wise in the light of contemporary cultural problems. From this pragmatic perspective, he gives us what he feels is the essential proclamation.

Stewart contends that the New Testament church proclaimed that prophecy was fulfilled. In Jesus of Nazareth, in his words and deeds, his life and death and resurrection, the new age has arrived. Further, God exalted him and he will come again as judge. The proper conclusion is that the day of salvation has arrived. The kingdom has come. This creates the message. From this Stewart derives five principles that must be found in all evangelistic proclamation if it is true to the Scriptures. To begin, the proclaimer is called to declare the divine incarnation of Jesus Christ. The facts of the *kerygma* are historical facts. The doctrine of the incarnation means "God has come right into the midst of the tumult and the shouting of this world."[16] And the facts of the incarnation are not only historical, they are unique. The kingdom of God, no less, has broken into the here and now. That is unique and unrepeatable and needs proper emphasis, especially today.

The evangelist also proclaims forgiveness. This is always relevant, for as Stewart states, "Whenever the Church truly proclaims the forgiveness of sins there the healing ministry is veritably at work."[17] The feeling of meaninglessness in life, so characteristic of our postmodern existentially oriented society, must be recognized as essentially a problem of sin. Iniquity and rebellion against God are the ultimate culprits in the contemporary loss of identity and feeling of utter aloneness. As the church preaches forgiveness, it strikes right at the heart of pressing present-day problems. As Kierkegaard said, "I must repent myself back into the family, into the clan, into the race, back to God."[18] There are moral absolutes, although postmoderns question that reality. Sin is real and everyone needs the genuine forgiveness of God.

In the third place, Stewart states that the proclaimer preaches the cross. The temple veil, which kept people out of God's presence and shut God in, has been torn in two. The darkness and mystery of God's "wholly otherness" has now been flung open to all, and all can approach him. As Stewart expresses it, "The death of Christ gives me the very heart of the eternal, because it is not words at all, not even sublime prophetic utterance: it is an act, God's act, against which I can batter all my doubts to pieces. We preach Christ crucified, God's truth revealed."[19] In God's revelation, the cross speaks of atonement, guilt bearing, and propitiation. Moreover, the demonic forces of the universe were once and for all defeated. Christ has overcome the world. "We preach Christ crucified" (1 Cor. 1:23) is always to be the cry of the proclaimer of the gospel.

Fourth, the "hour cometh, and now is." The long expected hope has occurred. Christ has been raised. The church declares a resurrected, living Lord. "This is indeed the very core of the apostolic *kerygma*."[20] It became the theme of every Christian sermon in the first century and should be ours today. The fact of the bodily resurrection of Jesus was no mere appendix tacked on the end of the message. The resurrection stands as a cosmic event, not just a personal victory for our Lord. God shattered all history by this mighty creative act. The resurrection means the entire world can experience a glorious rebirth. Nothing need ever be the same again. Naturally, the apostolic message did not see Good Friday and Easter as two isolated events. They were always presented as one mighty stroke of God. Now time has been baptized into eternity; things on this side of time immersed in things on the other. Atonement and reconciliation rest on the resurrection. It became God's act of justification. "This is our gospel. For this is what Christianity essentially is, a religion of Resurrection."[21]

Finally, and in summary, Stewart declares that the evangelist simply shares Christ. The message is not a cold, conceptualized theology or philosophy. A Person is proclaimed. And what a Person he is—the Helper, Shepherd, Companion, Friend, Light and Bread of Life, our Paraclete. If Christianity is anything, it is an experience of a "vital relationship to a living Christ."[22] The core of Christianity is a relationship with the living Lord Jesus Christ. This is the great discovery that the postmodern world—all the world for that matter—needs to make. How different society would become if it truly understood all that this means!

Stewart thus wisely casts the *kerygma* in a pragmatic context. He applies all the essentials of the proclamation to living human situations. Surely this is what must be done in all evangelization. The whole church must thoroughly understand the message theologically, but it must always be related in terms that address the *kerygma* to real life as we find it. As stressed, contextualizing the gospel is essential. And we must never forget or minimize that the *entire* church shares in the task of declaring Christ.

Basic Truths

What is to be learned from these and other varied approaches to the *kerygma?* Two lessons seem vital. First, whether we take the more rigid view of men like Dodd or a more flexible approach like that of Green and Webster, a basic biblical content rests at the core of all evangelistic proclamation if it is biblical. Specific theological and historical realities must be clearly understood and declared in the presentation of the gospel. And these basic truths center in and around the person and work of Jesus Christ.

Second, and touching our immediate concerns, evangelistic communication must contain the full *kerygma* that is wisely contextualized if we expect God's full blessings on our evangelization. So much so-called evangelistic work today seems rather bereft of the full biblical content of the *kerygma.* Mere appeals to the imagination, emotions, or the use of clichés and generalizations are not what the New Testament presents as evangelism. Our theme must be "We preach Christ" in all our attempts to win people to Jesus. This applies to all kinds of evangelistic proclamation—personal witnessing, writing, or whatever.

Preaching Today

What can be said of formally preaching the *kerygma?* Can preaching be relevant to our hour? Can the preacher really appeal to the postmodern?

At a conference for theological professors, a university professor of education tried to point out the inadequacies of the lecture method of teaching. After the rather self-contradictory hour was over (it was a lecture), the speaker was asked privately if what he said about lecturing in the classroom applied to preaching in the church. The professor retorted that though he was a lay preacher himself and preached every Sunday, he was convinced of the irrelevance of formally addressing people from the pulpit. He said he felt the hour spent each Sunday listening to a sermon was a virtual waste of time. What the distinguished professor said concerning preaching is not an uncommon attitude today, especially among postmoderns. Another speaker on the subject said:

> Preaching as such has fallen into disregard if not into disrepute. To local-
> ize this fact one could easily construct a historic chain of dominant Lon-
> don preachers from John Donne to Charles Haddon Spurgeon, who gen-
> eration after generation, in their immensely varied traditions, shaped and
> influenced the life of London. But somewhere, between Spurgeon and
> ourselves, the chain is broken.[23]

But after all, the critics tell us, we are in the age of television and the Internet. The general worldview of many has radically changed. We must have something new if we are to communicate effectively to people today. Forthright proclamation of the truth is out; dialogue is in, they tell us. The uneasy minds of postmoderns demand pictures, involve-ment, and discussion. Of course a real element of truth can be found in the argument. As one churchman has said, "Preaching is in the dol-drums, if not in the doghouse." Once the motto of Glasgow, Scotland, was: "Let Glasgow flourish through the preaching of the Word." Today the same city has on its promotional material simply "Let Glasgow flour-ish." What has happened to the preaching of the Word?

If such is the attitude about preaching in general, it is especially the case of evangelistic preaching in particular. Today many feel that preach-ing the gospel, as we traditionally understand that phrase, is almost an irrelevant exercise. Why try to preach evangelistically to those who have little or no idea what the preacher is talking about? Moreover, relatively few of those who need to hear the good news of Christ ever come to the church services.

The History of Preaching

The preaching enterprise boasts an illustrious history. As far back as Old Testament times, the preaching prophets stood head and shoulders above their peers. Hear Elijah thundering out judgment on Israel until even Ahab quaked! See the tearful Jeremiah preaching with such influ-ence that finally Zedekiah had him cast into a pit to stifle his voice! Or look at Elisha boldly addressing King Jehoram as he tells the monarch to send Naaman to him that all may know there is a prophet in Israel! And thrilling stories grew out of the preaching of Amos, Isaiah, the mys-tical Ezekiel, and their fellow prophets. Viewing the old dispensation, one thing is certain and stands out in bold relief: The preaching of the prophets had a profound influence on every aspect of the Israelite nation.

The New Testament era saw no change in emphasis; preaching remained paramount. In fact preaching came into its own in the apostolic age. Preaching in the early church held a central role in the divine mission. Who could deny, for example, the centrality and profound influence of the preaching of John the Baptist? All Jerusalem went out to the desert to hear him. Look into the ministry of the Lord himself. It has been said, "The great work of Christ during his life was preaching."[24] Perhaps this is to overstate the case, but obviously preaching was a very significant part of Jesus' ministry. Our Lord's own testimony was that he came "to bear witness to the truth" (John 18:37 RSV). It was natural, therefore, that the apostles and early disciples would follow the same tradition. Whether it was Peter at Pentecost, Philip in Samaria, or Paul in philosophical Athens, the power of proclamation was skillfully employed and the impact proved profound.

The church fathers were no exception to the rule; they too were great preachers. One still marvels at the impact of men like Augustine, Athanasius, and others through the centuries of church history. It was said of John Chrysostom that it would be better for the sun never to rise on Constantinople than for Chrysostom to stop preaching. Even in the Middle Ages, great preaching was not entirely lost. Bernard of Clairvaux preached so persuasively that mothers would lock their sons in the house to restrain them from following the monk back to the monastery. Francis of Assisi, though excelling in many Christian attributes, always considered himself first of all a preacher.[25]

Entering the Reformation period, preaching blossomed out on a scale not known for many years. No one questions the fact that preaching was a vital and essential factor in the entire Reformation movement. Men like Martin Luther, John Calvin, and John Knox were not only great theologians and writers, they became convincing preachers as well. Had these men and their colleagues not been persuasive proclaimers of their doctrine, one wonders what would have become of the Protestant Reformation.

After the ministries of preachers like William Perkins, William Ames, and John Bunyan, the eighteenth century dawned and brought the advent of another era of great preaching. The names of John Wesley, George Whitefield, and Jonathan Edwards are still well known. As these men preached, spiritual awakenings broke out. The next century was also a time of great preaching. Thousands flocked Sunday after Sunday to hear the oratory of pastors like C. H. Spurgeon, John Clifford, Phillips Brooks, and Henry Ward Beecher. Simultaneously, revivalists were preaching to large crowds. Charles Finney, Dwight Moody, John Wilbur Chapman, R. A. Torrey, and a host of others won thousands, even millions, to Christ. And where would the modern missionary movement be if it were not for the great preachers of the eighteenth and nineteenth centuries, men like William Carey, Judson Rice, and Hudson Taylor?

Even the twentieth century has not been bereft of effective preaching, despite the current downgrading of the practice. Billy Sunday, notwithstanding his weaknesses, is credited with winning a million people to faith in Christ. And no man in church history has preached to more people than Billy Graham. Moreover, there are men of God this very day who are filling their churches with worshipers, including postmoderns, who come to hear the Word of God preached in the power of the Holy Spirit.

In the light of a long and significant history, can preaching really be passé? One can seriously question that assumption. True, most postmoderns consider the revolutionary communication capabilities of television, the Internet, and computers as their primary, if not only, source of information. Yet, at the same time, a face on television or the Internet is not the same as a real human face in a dynamic person-to-person encounter permeated by God's Spirit. There is a substantial difference between a TV screen and a human face. And regardless of how lifelike digital stereo sound may be, it can never be as real as a genuine human voice. As we seek to proclaim the message, we must never forget that people relate in depth only with people. And preaching is just that—people relating to each other. As Phillips Brooks said, preaching is the communication of divine truth through personality to persons.

Of course, this does not mean we do not employ modern technology in getting the gospel before people. Let us use all means of communication. But God has honored and used preaching since the expulsion of Adam and Eve from the garden. For since sin came into the world at that moment, the preaching of forgiveness and salvation has become essential. It hardly seems likely that the Holy Spirit will lay it aside because of modern technology or a shift in society's worldview. In the course of human history, preaching has weathered every storm and still stands as a vital exercise in gospel propagation. Therefore, I boldly conclude that the days of preaching God's Word are not over. A revival of effective preaching is not unthinkable at all. Evangelistic preaching can still be effective. This certainly does not mean that we should retreat into the false security of living in the past. And it does not imply that we should disregard modern methods of communication that technical progress has given us. Moreover, relational evangelism—establishing a personal relationship with the postmodern unbeliever and presenting a convincing apologetic—is most important. Still, preaching can come alive even in our day. Preaching, yes, evangelistic preaching, can be effective in winning others to faith in Christ. As we develop "go-structures," that is, leaving the confines of a church building and going out to minister in the marketplaces of life, we can still find a real place for the pure preaching of the gospel. The church does not face an either/or choice of going to them or their coming to us. The wise church will develop every kind of evangelistic activity. But if we are to preach Christ with effect today, the church must take a fresh look at the entire preaching enterprise.

Prerequisites of Effective Evangelistic Preaching

Three things seem absolutely necessary to communicative preaching today, especially evangelistic preaching. If preaching is to regain its historical role, these principles are vital. First, the content of the proclamation is central. For evangelistic preaching (or any form of evangelistic communication) to be successful, there must be a clear-cut, positive presentation of the biblical gospel of Jesus Christ, and that means the full gospel, not mere summaries of it.

Second, effective, communicative methodology is essential. Here is where awareness of the preaching situation assumes a paramount role. If there is to be any hope for a positive response, the preacher must communicate in a way that makes sense to the hearer. Preachers must get to know postmoderns, understand them, and address them on their level.

The final consideration is the preacher as a Christian. The preacher of the gospel must embody spiritual qualities as God's servant if the preaching is to be effective. Preaching is always the communication of divine truth through personality. Let us look at these general principles in some detail.

The Content of Evangelistic Preaching

Although one never appreciates the type of preaching that grows out of a bigoted and narrow dogmatism, there must be no "uncertain sound" from the pulpit when the gospel is proclaimed. As Webster reminds us:

> A mood of uncertainty about the heart of the Gospel, the Lord of the Church, and the Savior of the world, is unworthy of Christians and bodes ill for the future of missions if it is allowed to be encouraged or persists. Describing the first mission to Thessalonica St. Paul wrote: "When we brought you the Gospel, we brought it not in mere words but in the power of the Holy Spirit, and with strong conviction, as you know well" (1 Thess. 1:5 NEB). Christian, even theological, humility is not synonymous with vagueness.[26]

Hopefully, this principle has been made amply clear by now.

The Methodology of Effective Proclamation

As important and fundamental as the content of preaching is, this does not exhaust the principles of effective proclamation. As has been stressed, a proper grasp of the preaching situation is vital to the success of evangelistic declaration. The preaching situation includes the entire setting and what transpires in a meaningful evangelistic preaching experience. It must be realized that the activity of preaching means much more than merely conveying the content of the Christian faith. Preaching Christ is a unique activity. It becomes an event, an event wherein God himself actually meets and addresses people personally. As H. H. Farmer has put it:

> Preaching is telling me something. But it is not merely telling me something. It is God actively probing me, challenging my will, calling me for decision, offering one His succor, through the only medium which the nature of His purpose permits Him to use, the medium of a personal relationship. It is as though, to adopt the Apostle's words, "God did beseech me by you." It is God's "I-thou" relationship with me carried on your "I-thou" relationship with me, both together coming out of the heart of His saving purpose which is moving on through history to its consummation in His Kingdom.[27]

Right there the distinctive nature of effective evangelistic preaching surfaces. Preaching in one sense can even be seen as something of a sacrament. Preaching is distinctively Christian preaching only insofar as it is both uttered and listened to *in faith*. In other words, baffling as it may seem, true preaching becomes God's activity—God encountering the hearers in the extreme and supreme crises of their lives and inspiring and generating faith. Real preaching therefore depends on the preacher's conveying the sense of the living, saving activity of God in Christ. It should be understood that the distinction between *kerygma* and *didache* is not to imply that the two never blend.

The preacher in the pulpit can communicate all the truth of God. And a layman in dialogue with one other person can surely be in the same spirit. *Kerygma* is not to be understood as always a monologue, nor is *didache* always dialogue. And as emphasized above, declaring God's Word is always to be done in faith and heard in faith. This implies that all genuine Christian communication always precipitates an encounter with the Holy Spirit, whether it is *kerygma* or *didache*.

These principles of Christian preaching indicate a number of things. Initially, as implied, preaching must always be viewed as personal encounter. God confronts people in the preaching situation on a Person-to-person level. As Farmer expressed it, "God's 'I-thou' relationship with me is never apart from, is always in a measure carried by, my 'I-thou' relationship with my fellows."[28] In this light one can see the position of the proclaimer.

In the first place, he or she must be intimately related to God in an "I-thou" sense. The Bible calls it abiding in Christ (John 15:4). If the proclaimer loses the reality of God's presence in preaching, all is lost. The preacher stands, as it were, at the right angle of a triangle, related vertically to God and horizontally to the hearers. In the context of this setting, God completes the triangle and confronts and addresses the needy hearers. That constitutes a true preaching situation. Moreover, there is give-and-take in all directions on the triangle. It becomes an existential encounter par excellence. As Donald Miller puts it:

> The Romanist says, When the priest pronounces the tremendous words of Consecration, he reaches up into the heavens, brings Christ down from his throne, and places him upon an altar to be offered up again as the victim for the sins of man. Protestantism, when it is true to its genius, does something better. When the Protestant preacher preaches—if he really preaches in the terms set forth here—the living Christ, who is always present in the fellowship of his people, both in heaven and on earth, expresses himself not in dumb symbol, but in living reality, and offers once again to men the reconciliation with God once accomplished by His death and resurrection and now eternally available to all who will believe. Men do not see through superstitious imagination and as mute observers a magical transformation of material symbols by the official intervention of a priest. They are confronted by the living Christ himself, who chooses to make his eternal redemptive Deed effectual by making the word of the preacher become His own word in the fellowship of the members of His body.[29]

The immediate implication of this kind of preaching is that a price has to be paid. The pulpit is not a place to be cool and casual in spirit and attitude. Effective proclamation does not come easily. The true preacher pours out himself. The relationship is a genuine encounter with people—people for whom Christ died—and with God. It can be an exhausting experience. Preaching can actually be painful when one gives of oneself, as one ought. Paul said, "Therefore be on the alert, remembering that night and day for a period of three years I did not cease to admonish each one with tears" (Acts 20:31).

Finally, let it be stressed once again that the preacher must always keep people in view during the preaching enterprise. In this age of uncertainty and loss of absolutes, this is most important. Preaching is to people as they are. To them we address our message in love, compassion, and understanding as we attempt to relate to them meaningfully. Biblical, life-situation preaching has become a must these days. Thus we conclude that the basic existential preaching situation described must be understood and cultivated, for this becomes the context in which God works.

The Preacher Himself

A word about the preacher who declares God's message is needed. Dr. Raymond Brown reminds us that the effective preacher today must embody three essential qualities. First, the preacher must be a person of acute observation. It takes more than just understanding the Scriptures to be a preacher relevant to today's postmodern world. We must be students of society. We must know our world, no matter what form of evangelization in which we may engage—preacher, teacher, or personal witness. The late missiologist D. T. Niles said, "If we want to talk with God we had better find out something about the world because that is the only subject in which God is interested."[30] The same surely is true if we want to speak *for* God. Roger Schutz has correctly confessed that often "we allow ourselves to be caught up in a Christian environment that we find congenial and in the process create a ghetto of like-minded people who are quite unmindful of the real world."[31]

The preacher must also be a compassionate listener. As Brown puts it, we must "learn again to listen." The preacher must listen on a twofold level, first to God and then to people. God's spokesperson speaks for God to the real needs of real people. How can we effectively communicate unless there is a genuine openness to both? We must get out of ivory towers or religious ghettos. Ezekiel had it right when he said, "I sat where they sat, and remained there astonished among them" (Ezek. 3:15 KJV). That was where the prophet learned to be God's spokesperson.

And the preacher must be a discerning teacher. This is obvious. If ever there was a day of alarming ignorance concerning the Word of God, this is that day. May God make of his spokesmen those who are faithfully "holding forth the word of life; that I may rejoice in the day of Christ, that I have not run in vain, neither laboured in vain" (Phil. 2:16 KJV). And all these principles hold true for the informal personal witness just as for formal preaching.

It can be said by way of summary that the preaching evangelist or personal witness must simply be a true disciple of Jesus Christ, one who walks with God in the Spirit's fullness. The effective proclaimer knows by experience, daily experience, the One whose message is proclaimed. As Farmer has well said, "I suppose in the end the secret lies in the quality of our own spiritual life and the extent to which we are ourselves walking humbly with God in Christ."[32] I will say more about these principles in chapter 9.

Coming to the final section on the theme of proclaiming the gospel, a look into the actual evangelistic service itself may prove helpful.

The Evangelistic Service

Why do we find a measure of disillusionment today concerning evangelistic services, especially in the local church? Several misconceptions or problems seem responsible for tending to make pulpit evangelism less attractive than it used to be. Apparently some pastors have been hesitant to give a whole service over to evangelism because of the relatively few unbelievers who normally attend the worship services of the church. But there are still some there. And these, if only a few, need to hear the gospel preached. Moreover, there may well be more unbelievers attending the average church on any given Sunday than realized. Simply because most present are church members does not necessarily mean all are truly regenerate believers. Billy Graham said that in America the greatest evangelistic opportunity could probably be found in the churches themselves. An alarming number of church members show scant evidence of a true redemptive experience of Christ. Furthermore, if pastors will faithfully develop good evangelistic services and forthrightly preach the gospel, the Holy Spirit will surely honor the effort and bring unbelievers to hear the Good News. Not only that, outreaching church members can greatly help the pastor by bringing to church worship services friends who need Christ. It should be an entire congregational activity, a challenge kept before the believers. This personal effort can be an important aspect of relational evangelism.

A second problem centers in the fact that some pastors tend to restrict their pulpit evangelism to just a short word of encouragement to accept Christ at the end of almost any kind of sermon or service. This practice usually fails to get positive results. There is no substitute in evangelistic proclamation for the presentation of the full gospel, and an evangelistic service needs to be shaped with the aim of winning people to Christ; the worship must be "user friendly."

Then, there are preachers who for one reason or another in an evangelistic service fail to give an effective challenge to the unbeliever. Consequently, they see little result and are often disillusioned with preaching evangelistically. This practice can result from a misunderstanding of the appeal portion of the *kerygma*. That is, they may preach all about the Christ event but then fail to remember that the apostolic message called men and women then and there to repent and believe (Acts 20:21). As John Stott has expressed it, "We must never make the proclamation without then issuing an appeal."[33] Proclaimers need to become exhorters and give a forthright challenge. And remember, the response is not up to the preacher; conversion is God's work. The preacher's role is merely to challenge the hearers. The response comes by the Holy Spirit, and he can be counted on to act. Timidity thus has no place in evangelistic preaching. The proclaimer has no reputation to keep or build as Christ's ambassador. Of course, the type of invitation given should be of the nature that suits the situation. No one method suffices for all contexts. But surely the Holy Spirit can guide his servants in how to be relevant in evangelization.

Probably the prime reason some pastors and leaders view the evangelistic service as relatively ineffective today is that they feel inadequate and/or uninstructed on just how to develop a sound, sane, and spiritual evangelistic thrust in the context of a worship service that is relevant to today's world. But in such a high and holy venture, who does feel fully competent? We are human. Still, a few suggestions can perhaps help if one aspires to win people to Christ through preaching.

Simple Principles

Let the preacher first of all have confidence in the fact that, as George Sweazey states, the "pulpit still offers the minister his supreme evangelistic opportunity. No form of communication the Church has ever found compares with preaching."[34] Even if Sweazey has somewhat overstated the case, the evangelistic preaching service has an important role in mission. Let us have the full assurance of faith that God can and will use this methodology. If this is true, certain disciplines must be followed.

First and foremost, there should be adequate preparation. This must be seen in a twofold sense. Initially, the proclaimer must be fully prepared. This includes spiritual, mental, and emotional preparation. With the essence of the *kerygma* in mind, the basic objective becomes winning people to faith in Christ. Great preaching is purposeful preaching. And of course spiritual preparation is vital so that one can fully expect God to bless the preaching of the Word. This spiritual and purposeful preparation does not come easily. Being truly prepared to preach has its price.

Preparation for an evangelistic service means preparing the people as well. A wise approach is to inform the church in some fashion that an evangelistic service is planned for a certain date. Enlist the people to pray, to bring unbelieving friends, and then to come expecting God to bless and to draw people to himself. The more effort and prayer that is put into such a service, the more one can anticipate that God will honor it.

Then it is vitally important that the proper atmosphere be developed in the actual service. This is essentially the work of the Holy Spirit, but there are a number of things God may use to create such an atmosphere. There should be something contagiously dynamic about the entire service, for we are proclaiming the Good News. The spirit of warmth, expectation, and joy that God's people exude is provoking in itself. A number of things go into creating this atmosphere. First, it is a time for relatively short prayers. The unbeliever will not follow long prayers. There is, to be sure, a time for longer prayers that comes before the service. Long periods of announcements are certainly not helpful. Further, the person who conducts the service should not be somber and slow. The whole service should move along smoothly and dynamically.

In an evangelistic service the right music is vital. It can almost make or break the effectiveness of the service. Music tastes change. We must be aware of the revolution going on in this area of worship. In many congregations the music needs a drastic updating. Edwin McNeely states: "It has been said many times that religion must sing or die . . . music . . . with its inherent emotional content, becomes a powerful force in drawing men into a proper relationship with God."[35] The hymns and/or choruses chosen should present the gospel in a positive, enjoyable, and singable fashion. And let's be up-to-date in all selections, at least as much as possible. The time is overdue for music based on the language of an urbanized, postmodern society rather than that of rural nostalgia. Not too many people go to "the little brown church in the vale" anymore. Music that communicates the true message of Christ in the words and phrases that are meaningful to current mentality and thought structure is vital if we aspire to reach people.

Here is an area for much thought and prayer. This does not mean that all the older hymns are outmoded by any means. John Newton's "Amazing Grace" made the pop charts a few years ago. The rich truth of Christ does communicate. And songs should have good Bible content—let us use music that says something, but a continuing updating of hymnology is always needed. This has been true through centuries of church life.

Further, special music must be employed effectively, with skillful use of choirs, soloists, groups, and instrumentalists. Parker said, "I believe that there is as much conviction lodged in the mind by singing as by preaching."[36] Thus it appears most wise for the worship leaders to give serious, imaginative attention to the music phase of the service—and to lead the more traditionally minded church member to recognize changing realities.

In developing an effective evangelistic service, little probably needs to be said about the actual preaching itself. This we have already discussed in some detail. The word of Andrew Blackwood concerning evangelistic preaching gets to the point: "As for the preaching, every sermon ought to glow. It should be a burning message from the heart of God to the man in the pew."[37] All, of course, must be guided and empowered by the Holy Spirit. He alone can lead and inspire his proclaimers in what to do and say. After all, as is so often said, it is all God's work. Again, that holds true for personal witnessing as well.

Finally, the leader who involves laypeople is wise. Testimonies, special music, drama, and so on can often be used to project the idea that the service is really of and for the people. Obviously this helps break down many barriers, making the service more "user friendly." The leaders must be imaginative in creating an evangelistic service. When a creative, dynamic service is developed and the gospel fully preached in the power of the Holy Spirit, God will honor it. Our Lord knows how to reach postmoderns. As the poet Henry Crocker put it:

> Give us a watchword for this hour.
> A thrilling word, a word of power,
> A battle-cry, a flaming breath
> That calls to conquest or to death.
> A word to rouse the Church from rest
> To heed her Master's high request.
> The call is given, you hosts, arise,
> Our watchword is evangelize.[38]

But there is more. Effective evangelism emerges out of a strong theological base. That issue must be addressed.

Questions and Issues for Study

1. What is the essence of the gospel?
2. Why is it vital to share the *whole* gospel with people?
3. Why does the gospel have such power?
4. What must one do to communicate the gospel to postmoderns?
5. What aspect of the gospel is most difficult to get across to postmoderns?
6. How does one deal with the sin issue?

7. How do you eliminate the obstacles raised against the gospel?
8. How does the Holy Spirit work in communicating the gospel?
9. What is the goal of everyone—preacher, teacher, witness—in declaring Christ?
10. What are *you* going to do about proclaiming the Good News?

six

A Basic Theology
of Evangelism

If the church would effectively evangelize today's postmodern world, it must do so from a strong theological base. We have seen the essential theology of the gospel *(kerygma)*, but a broader perspective must be grasped so as to lay a foundation for the entire evangelistic enterprise. It has been quite correctly stated that "there can be no effective and permanent evangelism without theology, and there would soon be few persons ready to study theology without evangelism."[1] If evangelism loses sight of basic, biblical theology, it does so at its own peril. And it goes without saying that theology divorced from the fervor of evangelism is superficial and faulty. It cannot be stated too strongly that the two disciplines, when separated, part to their mutual detriment.

Reasons for Uniting Theology and Evangelism

Several sound reasons arise as to why theology and mission must not be separated, the first and by far the most important being that they are never divorced in the Scriptures. This is evident by the simple fact that the books of the New Testament were not composed primarily as dissertations on Christian theology; rather, they were the "incidental literature of evangelism."[2] For example, many of Paul's most profound doctrinal statements grew out of an evangelistic and pastoral concern for the churches, for example, the Galatian letter. At the same time these books give us the very essence of our Christian theology. This stands to reason, for evangelism by its very name implies a theology. It is the Good News that God has revealed about himself. Thus it can be put in propositional form. It can be discussed, implications formulated, and doctrines created. Moreover, evangelistic passion grows out of rich doctrinal understanding. And that is important for the gospel.

A second reason for the uniting of theology and mission is that without sound theological content, evangelism soon degenerates into sentimentalism, emotionalism, and gimmicks. Such charges have at times been directed toward the evangelistically minded. Sadly enough, all too often there is substance to the criticisms. And it is rather dishonest—and may even betray a simple laziness—for the evangelical to retort that such a charge on the part of the critic grows out of spiritual coldness and a lack of concern for the unbelieving world. Any form of evangelism that resorts to the manipulation of people, regardless of the motive, is unworthy of the gospel. Even more tragically, such a use of evangelism can lead unsuspecting and honest inquirers into a shallow understanding that falls short of a genuine experience of salvation. Scriptural evangelism demands that the evangelist fill the presentation of the gospel with solid theological content. That price must be paid if God's approval of the work is to be expected, for people are rarely if ever genuinely converted by psychological maneuvering, persuasive oratory, or emotional stories devoid of the impact of the Holy Spirit. For the sake of those whom we would reach for Christ, authentic theology and evangelism must not be separated. We must avoid superficial "believeism."

The third reason for fusing theology and evangelism rests in the pragmatic fact that God has honored most profoundly the ministry of those who do. A mere cursory survey of the history of mission clearly demonstrates this truth. The early church fathers are a patent example. Augustine of Hippo in the fourth and fifth centuries was a great theologian. His system of thought was foundational in his own day and had significant influence on the Reformers a millennium later. Yet he also served as a very effective evangelist. His great work *City of God* was inspired directly by the spirit of mission. Concerning Christian theology, Augustine said it "must be carried into practice, and . . . taught for the very purpose of being practiced . . . ; the preacher must sway the mind so as to subdue the will."[3] He demonstrated in his ministry that beautiful blend of sound biblical theology and evangelism.

Illustrations of this type can be multiplied over and over again in the lives of men like Calvin, Luther, Arminius, Wesley, and Whitefield. In more recent times the principle is seen in evangelists like Charles Finney, the great American preacher of the nineteenth century whose ministry won thousands while he was also teaching theology at Oberlin College for more than forty years. R. A. Torrey, a very successful evangelist, became a highly competent student; he read his polyglot Bible every day. And a number of our own contemporaries who follow this tradition could be mentioned. One can thus conclude from a purely practical perspective that God uses most significantly the person who blends evangelistic ministry with a sound theology. C. E. Autrey declared:

> Theology is to evangelism what the skeleton is to the body. Remove the skeleton and the body becomes a helpless quivering mass of jelly-like substance. By means of the skeleton the body can stand erect and move. The great systems of theological truths form the skeleton which enables our revealed religion to stand.[4]

People deserve to hear the *full* truth of Jesus Christ and salvation.

Other reasons could be given for the necessity of a strong theology for effective evangelism. For example, a knowledge of theology helps make the presentation of the gospel message plain; it makes the evangelist more sure of his message; a genuine understanding of the rich content of the Bible will fill one with zeal; theology is an important agent in conserving evangelistic results. The major reasons given above should convince any Christian who seeks to win unbelievers that theology and mission must be forever wed.

Formulating a Theology of Evangelism

Therefore, the evangelist of any type must formulate a strong theology of evangelism. Space will obviously preclude any attempt to present a thoroughgoing doctrinal presentation of mission. It may even appear a bit presumptuous to give only one chapter to a theme that can boast volumes. Yet there are basic truths that a person must make ingredients of his or her life of outreach if he or she hopes to be effective in evangelistic activity. So I shall be brave and briefly discuss in a simple, straightforward fashion, several essential aspects of a theology of evangelism. They are all time-honored truths of Jesus Christ. However, we can become so familiar with them that we tend to fall into the trap that J. H. Jowett called, "the deadening familiarity with the sublime." We need to grasp the incredible depths of these realities, even though they seem so familiar to us. Remember, they are not familiar to the unbeliever; and when understood, they are revolutionary.

The Necessity of Christian Conversion

It appears obvious that the biblical presentation of the necessity of conversion lays the first foundation stone in building a theology of evangelism. It may seem to some quite unnecessary even to approach such an axiomatic doctrine. Yet today the need of conversion is implicitly, if not explicitly, being more and more called into question. The growing spirit of syncretism and universalism is being felt even in circles that have been traditionally evangelical and evangelistic. This is especially true among the younger generation. They display a deep desire for spirituality, but they ask why *Christian* conversion is *absolutely* essential. It becomes increasingly vital to make clear the need of *Christian* conversion. To a greater or lesser degree, everyone recognizes the reality of personal sin and the need of a change in lifestyle. But Christian understandings differ dramatically from *all* other world religions, philosophers, and ideas as to how the sin issue can be settled. All but the Christian worldview essentially take the track of self-effort as the answer. Even perversions of the Jewish faith assume this stance, hence our Lord's encounters with the scribes and Pharisees and Paul's conflicts with the Judaizers (Gal. 2:15–16). The Christian gospel emphatically declares that forgiveness, conversion, and eternal life come purely by grace through faith (Eph. 2:8–10). By the "works of the Law" no one is justified in God's righteous eyes. That is a radical difference from what other religions teach and a vital necessity. Thus we stress the centrality of Christian conversion. Only through this experience is one brought into fellowship with God. We may need to first present an apologetic to the postmodern, but they must be led to see the centrality of Christian conversion for a meaningful life—not to mention eternity.

The necessity of Christian conversion can be seen in the scriptural doctrine of sinful humanity. As is often said, to understand the Good News of God, we must first understand the bad news of people.[5] Appropriately, therefore, in the early chapters of Genesis we have the account of the creation of man and woman, their corruption by sin, and the consequences of willful disobedience to God's word of command. The Bible thereafter uses several figures to describe this rebellious state.

The corruption of the first man and woman has invaded the entire human race. We stand corrupted, blind, diseased, lost, and dead. These facts portray in bold relief the fact that something has gone terribly awry with human character. The Bible depicts clearly this perversion of our true humanity. Absolutely no scriptural warrant exists for holding the view that people are essentially good, even despite the fact that we are created in God's image (Rom. 7:18). All stand in desperate need. Everyone is in real trouble, and our trouble, as Culbert Rutenber has correctly said, lies in an utter "failure of relationships."[6]

Relationships Destroyed

No person is a mere object. No one is an atomic simple, that is, existing alone with no relationships. The human person can never be understood apart from life's essential relationships. These essential relationships, Rutenber tells us, are three—our relation to God, our relation to our fellows, and our relation to ourselves. We are related to God in that he made us for fellowship with himself. This constitutes the meaning of the "image of God." We are made in and for the love of God. This makes us responsible and human. Second, we all are related to others in a social sense. No one can be "an island entirely to himself alone." Interhuman relationships form a vital part of that which makes life what it is. Finally, we are related to ourselves. We can talk to ourselves, think about ourselves; in a word, we have self-consciousness. Moreover, we can forge our own character and personality. And right there sin does its destructive work.

Sin Corrupts Life's Relationships

When we are disobedient to God, all of life's basic relationships are corrupted. Sin bludgeons every important tie that makes life worth living and truly human, as God intended in creation. To begin with, sin in the divine-human relationship causes a sense of guilt—genuine guilt, not just neurotic guilt feelings. Sin centers in a refusal to let God act in our life. This makes us truly guilty before God. Guilt feelings inevitably arise. They should—we are guilty and condemned. Judgment—eternal judgment—is our lot, for the essential God-human relationship has been corrupted.

In the second place, sin in relation to our fellows precipitates a spirit of lovelessness. The only thing that holds the structures of society together in harmony is love. When love degenerates, society, with its vital human relationships, crumbles. Little wonder that the world languishes in the condition it's in today! With love gone, only selfishness remains, even though it may be cultured or restrained by law.

Lastly, sin in relation to self spells bondage, perversion, frustration, and depression. Self-relatedness becomes corrupted by evil just as surely as in the other essential relationships of life. A person can be himself or herself only when properly related to God and others. As Rutenber graphically describes it: "With God lost, I am thrown back on myself to live off my own nerves and feed off my own fingernails."[7]

Thus sin perverts all of life; we struggle in guilt, lovelessness, and bondage. Though sin and rebellion mean more, perhaps much more than this, it should at least be clear that everyone stands in desperate need of drastic change. A more honest look at society today should make that reality crystal clear, and a little straightening up here and there will never do. We stand in need of radical, revolutionary change. Each of us needs to become a whole new person. The entire system of relationships cries out to be healed, longing for reconciliation at a profound level.

We actually need to die and start over again, and that is just what conversion means. It is a turn that utterly transforms life. It can be described as dying and being raised from the dead, exactly what occurs in Christian conversion. Paul said, "I have been crucified with Christ; and it is no longer I who live, but Christ lives in me; and the life which I now live in the flesh I live by faith in the Son of God, who loved me and gave Himself up for me" (Gal. 2:20). This is our only hope, and only Christ can accomplish it. This is why we contend so vigorously for the absolute necessity of true Christian conversion.

Scripture calls for genuine repentance and faith, for this alone brings about a true conversion experience. The Bible is unmistakably clear in its demands for such an in-depth exercise of the will. As Michael Green, in his excellent work *Evangelism in the Early Church*, has said,

> although it [salvation] is absolutely universal in its offer, Mark knows that the good news is only effective among those who repent, believe, and are prepared to engage in costly, self-sacrificial discipleship. Only the man who is prepared to lose his life for the sake of Christ and the gospel can find it; for it was only in losing his life for the sake of others that Christ could offer a new life to men, the new life proclaimed in the gospel.[8]

In the light of these scriptural truths, it seems strange that some try to downgrade the inescapable necessity of a radical conversion experience for all people. Perhaps it grows out of a misunderstanding of the nature or message of the Bible or a shallow grasp of the real condition of people without Christ. It seems very unlikely that many will be zealous in evangelistic labors until they are utterly convinced of these facts and experience the compassion of Christ concerning the depth of humanity's plight. Surely these truths are vital to a dynamic theology of evangelism.

This leads us to investigate what God has done to remedy humanity's awful sickness.

God as Redeemer

As has been seen, the Scriptures paint a dark and somber picture of human sin. But God's Word also paints a bright portrait of Jesus Christ as the Redeemer and Reconciler. The whole Bible is saying clearly and forcefully that God redeems; that is, he transforms our lives by saving us from our sins.

God redeems as Father. He desires all to become his children, so he sent his Son. He reveals himself as Father, for he desires that we live in that relationship. He is King, and he wishes everyone to submit to his authority. He is the giver of life, desiring all to receive its fullness. Above all, he is love, and so he pleads with us to receive his love and walk in a fellowship of love with himself.

God redeems as Son. This is obvious; the Good News is news about the Son. The entire Christ event is all about redemption. The essence of the incarnation centers in this fact. Because Jesus Christ came as a man and at the same time was the Son of God, he was able to do what was necessary for all humanity. The mystery that Jesus Christ is all man and all God makes the cross and resurrection efficacious for all. The cross and resurrection cry out *redemption,* from the first blow of the hammer in piercing his hand to the cry of "It is finished" to the glad announcement "He is risen." All is salvation. The poet said it well: "In my place condemned He stood. Sealed my pardon with His blood. Hallelujah! What a Saviour." Further, the resurrection means a new redeemed life. The Christian experience is a perpetual Easter. Little wonder Paul wrote, "We preach Christ" (1 Cor. 1:23).

God redeems as Holy Spirit. He convinces of sin, righteousness, and judgment (John 16:7–11). He alone can reveal Christ and inspire and create faith. He becomes the agent in the entire regeneration experience (John 3:5, 8), sealing for eternity the newborn Christian (Eph. 1:13). New life is imparted as he comes to abide as God in the human life and thus makes the human body the temple of God (1 Cor. 6:19). He transforms the believer into a truly different person by forming Christ within (Gal. 4:19). Apart from the working of the Holy Spirit, there is no personal redemption. The Holy Spirit makes the Lord Jesus Christ one's constant contemporary.

We conclude that all three persons of the triune Godhead are utterly involved in the sinner's reconciliation. Therefore, we can have confidence in the atonement of Jesus Christ.

Confidence in the Atonement

Concerning the atonement, the saving work of Christ, more detailed attention is demanded. Grasping the meaning of the atonement is essential to a sound theology of evangelism, for from this we develop confidence in the reconciling work of Jesus Christ that will motivate us to proclaim fearlessly and joyously its tremendous truths.

There was a time when much interest was given to the various so-called theories of the atonement. Theologians would elucidate each concept in some detail and then discuss at length its various merits and defects. Space, if not contemporary interest, forbids such a detailed exercise here, but it may still prove helpful to see at least the salient contribution the different theories have given to our understanding of the work of Christ. It should broaden our grasp of the message of salvation.

The governmental or substitutionary theory, defended by many, if not all, evangelicals, tells us that Christ came and died essentially as a substitute for us. He stood in our place and bore our penalty. It views the atonement as a satisfaction of God's justice. The law and its demands had to be met, and Christ accomplished this when he died in our place and bore our judgment in himself. In the act of Christ's death and resurrection—they must be viewed as one—God's just law was met and he was satisfied. Here is a basic aspect of the truth to be fully understood and forthrightly proclaimed in the presentation of the gospel. We are pardoned because Christ, Son of God and Son of Man, bore our punishment.

The example (Socinian) theory states that by Christ's death on the cross, lost and alienated people are motivated to reconcile themselves to God. The weakness of this approach rests in its failure to grasp the fact that God, because of our sin, must also be seen as reconciled to us in the work of Christ as well as the converse. Vincent grasped this truth when he spoke of God's "transformed face" toward sinners.

But at least the theory does point out, and quite correctly, that we all desperately need reconciling to God, that the basic divine-human relationship needs to be restored. Further, it points to the fact that the death of Christ presents a beautiful example of faithfulness to truth, duty, love, and mercy; thus it has a powerful influence on our own moral improvement. Christ's example of compassion and sacrifice should kindle a response in us. Of course, the cross is far more than example, yet it surely is that also. The so-called *Bushnellian or moral influence theory* has much the same approach with its attendant failings and strong points.

The impact of the *commercial (Anselmic) theory* rests in its grasp of the fact that the divine honor is grossly sinned against in humanity's rebellion. The consequences are that eternal punishment must attend the offender. But this approach suffers from a lack of understanding that more than the divine honor is at stake in our sin. For example, divine honor cannot become more prominent than divine holiness. Still, one must grant that God's honor was involved in it all, and in that sense the concept has something to say.

The dramatic theory emphasizes the struggle between the forces of God and the forces of evil. In one sense this tends to leave people somewhat out of the picture in its stress on the struggle of opposing forces, even though we were deeply involved in the whole affair. The Bible does clearly declare that a great battle was being waged and the forces of evil, as epitomized in the devil and demons and the "world," were routed and destroyed in the Christ event. Jesus did "overcome the world" (John 16:33) and all that implies, and Satan was cast out (Luke 10:18).

The ransom theory, sometimes called the patristic view, is something of a variation of the above concept. The idea revolves around the concept that if we were redeemed through a ransom paid by God, the one who was paid must have been Satan. Few hold such a morally repugnant view today; although Gustaf Aulen, in his *Christus Victor,* proposes something of a demythologized version of the concept. True, our salvation was very costly to God, but he did not pay a ransom to the devil or anyone to purchase freedom for captive men and women. The truth to be stressed in the concept of a ransom paid is that the atonement price was the costly blood of Christ, and God who paid that price is thus the great Deliverer. We shall expand this in more detail when later in this chapter we consider the idea of justification.

A. H. Strong brings several of the strengths of these views together in the approach he conceived and called *the ethical theory.* He makes the following points: (1) the atonement must be seen as rooted in the holiness of God; (2) it must answer the ethical demands of the divine nature; (3) in the humanity of Christ and his sufferings all claims of justice are met; (4) atonement was accomplished through the solidarity of the race; (5) it satisfies humanity's ethical needs; (6) the atonement is for all, but all must avail themselves of it.

Now what can be said about all these various approaches to the atonement? Whether or not we agree with all that the various thinkers assert, it is important to glean from the various theories any aspects of truth and then incorporate them into a full system. This approach has obvious value, for the atonement is a many-faceted jewel; yet we must say that the "core" of the jewel rests in the substitutionary view. But to fix one's gaze on just one facet is to neglect the beauty of the whole. So pro-

found is the scriptural presentation of the atonement, a completely satisfying theology is most difficult, if not impossible, to construct. The
more we look into the wonders of the atonement, the more glorious it
becomes. As we continue our gaze, we will discover new wonders that
we must pass on to others. At the same time, as we have said, as each
theory becomes a facet of the jewel of truth, the primary essence rests
in the fact that Christ died and rose as the divine Substitute, and in that
great act of grace, God was satisfied. This must be stressed.

There are other, modern, quite unique interpretations of the atonement. These may be of interest but must be left for more critical studies. Now perhaps a brief excursion into some of the various biblical
terms that describe salvation will help us in gaining a deeper understanding and more profound confidence in the saving work of Christ.

Some Key Words

Conversion

A term we have already used several times is *conversion*. The necessity of conversion has been discussed, but a closer look at the etymol-
ogy of the word itself should prove helpful. The New Testament word-
group is based on the Greek word *epistrephein*. As might be expected,
this word-group is used in classical and Koine Greek alike in a nonthe-
ological sense. It means simply "to turn," as to turn a ship or to turn
oneself around. It can also connote "to turn the mind" or "turn one's
attention to." Etymologically this led to the usage "to warn, to correct,
to cause to repent." Thus we see it acquiring religious overtones. Quite
naturally, therefore, the New Testament writers picked it up, as it seemed
ideally suited to present the concept behind salvation. In the New Testament Scriptures themselves, the word-group in its substantial and ver-
bal forms is used some thirty-five times. It is rarely used in a transitive
sense except in Luke 1:17 and James 5:19–20. Frequently it can be found
used in a physical sense of turning or returning, for example, Matthew
12:44 and Luke 2:39. But for our immediate interest, the biblical writers employed it most to connote a mental or spiritual turn. Classic examples are Peter's call to repentance in Acts 3:19 and the account of Acts
9:35 where many "turned" to the Lord.

The Old Testament equivalent, *shubh*, occurs some 1,146 times and is
used in much the same fashion as the *epistrephein* word-group. The basic
theological idea in both Testaments is this: God calls one to turn, to change
the direction of thinking, affections, will, and so on. It implies a complete
reversal of all of life. This indicates that the repentant turns from some-

thing to something. A person turns from himself or herself to God. As Emil Brunner has expressed it, repentance is coming alive to one's true self as a sinner, and faith is coming to God as a Savior. This is conversion.

Redemption

Another central idea in salvation is conveyed in the word *redemption,* a common word in current theological writings. The wide use of the term should be seen as a relatively modern development. The New Testament uses the word rather sparingly, and theologians normally followed that pattern until relatively recent times. When the word was employed by older writers, it tended to be used in a rather restricted sense. The man in the street of the first century thought of it in a completely nonreligious sense, such being the case with many of the terms that now have deep theological implications. The basic word is *lutron*—"to ransom, or to loose." It was used to describe almost any kind of loosing, like the loosing of people from prison. However, in such a case, when one was loosed as a prisoner of war, for example, a ransom price was paid. Hence the concept of release on receipt of ransom grew up around the term. As Leon Morris points out, "this idea of payment as the basis of release . . . is the reason for the existence of the whole word-group."[9]

So we can see that the basic biblical concept of redemption is the paying of a ransom price to secure a liberation. However, when God is the subject of the verb, a shift of emphasis occurs. Morris correctly states that God alone could pay a ransom to redeem sinners, and surely not to the devil as the old ransom theory of the atonement holds. The stress must be placed on the idea of deliverance rather than on the means by which God brought it about. At the same time, the truth arises that God delivers his people at a cost, a high cost. We know of course that the cost was the precious blood of Christ (1 Peter 1:18–19). Consequently, "believers are not brought by Christ into a liberty of selfish ease. Rather, since they have been bought by God at terrible cost, they have become God's slaves, to do His will."[10] Postmoderns—and all—need to know this. Moreover, a proper understanding and declaration of this tremendous truth should save us from a shallow evangelism.

Justification

It would appear that the dominating idea in Paul's concept of salvation can be found in the word *justification.* This is true if one can judge from the sheer number of times he employs the term. The word-group from which it derives is *dikaios*—"righteous." The basic idea is a "proper standing before God." It describes the status of righteousness conferred by God on the basis of the work of Christ in his death and resurrection. Emphasis must be laid on the idea of imputation, for there is no sense in which such a status can be attained by human works of righteousness.

The root of the doctrine can be found in the Old Testament view of righteousness. God in his holiness demands full righteousness among all peoples. The law clearly demonstrates this fact. Many Jews strove to fulfill the requirement by performing deeds of legal righteousness. This was a basic blunder, for they could never attain perfection.

The New Testament presents the whole concept clearly as *imputed* righteousness. People sin and cannot be righteous in themselves, but Christ died for all and fulfilled the demands of the law in our stead. The forensic idea is paramount. Classical evangelicalism has always interpreted the idea to mean that Christ endured the penalty of sin that the eternal law of righteousness could be fulfilled. As Calvin put it, "As the law allowed no remission, and God did remit sins, there appeared to be a stain on divine justice. The exhibition of Christ as an atonement is what alone removes it."[11]

So a person is justified, declared righteous in God's sight, when he or she exercises faith in the atoning work of Christ. Grace through faith opens up this new status. The forensic implications of the concept thus become clear, and our communicating of the gospel should make this essential element of the truth plain. Of course, when the new life of Christ is embraced, the Holy Spirit begins his sanctifying work to make us more ethical and moral—more "righteous" in our personal lives. But that is because we are now accepted as righteous before God because of Christ's imputed righteousness.

Reconciliation

It may well be that the most relevant aspect of salvation to our postmodern day centers in the truths implied by the word *reconciliation*. It has already been pointed out in some detail that we all live in a threefold relationship—to God, our fellows, and ourselves. The rupturing of these vital relationships constitutes the tragedy of sin. Reconciliation means the restoring of these essential and vital relationships, and postmoderns zealously seek out relationships.

Rutenber points out that modern psychiatry is deeply involved with these three problems. The problems of guilt, inability to give and/or receive love, and lack of freedom to function properly in society occupy the counselor. But it is clear that the psychiatrist deals with them on an entirely different level than the Christian witness. And though the psychiatrist may remove neurotic guilt, real guilt remains; and though he or she may help a loveless neurotic give and receive love on a human level, only Christ can impart by his Holy Spirit the *agape* love of God; and though the doctor may aid a person to find release from fear so as to function more successfully as a useful member of society, only the new birth gives that person the true liberty of the children of God. In other words, "psychiatry and the gospel work on a man's problems on different though not unrelated levels. The well-integrated, well-adjusted, and socially well-manicured person still needs redemption."[12] And Christ's salvation provides just that. Here is a more in-depth look at these concepts.

First, one is reconciled to God, for salvation means forgiveness, real forgiveness for real sin. In Christ, God freely pardons us. True guilt before God and its attending feelings are eradicated. One can say with Paul, "We have peace with God through our Lord Jesus Christ" (Rom. 5:1 KJV). Moreover, through Christ's work in death and resurrection, God becomes genuinely reconciled to us. This theological truth must not be overlooked. Reconciliation is a two-way street. God has been offended and needs reconciliation to man. That too is accomplished in the Christ event.

The sinner must recognize God's moral prerogative to forgive justly in Christ, for before forgiveness becomes morally effective, the conscience and moral sense of the forgiven must be satisfied. Christ completely meets these demands, and Christian reconciliation with its marvelous peace is accomplished at two levels. The forgiven sinner knows God has not "leaned over backward" to forgive him. God remains just and yet the justifier of those who believe (Rom. 3:26). Forgiveness and reconciliation are offered in such a way that the forgiven one is not humiliated and his self-respect taken away. Moreover, the moral structure of the universe is safeguarded. As Rutenber has reminded us, "The cross makes forgiveness possible without making righteousness secondary."[13]

Reconciled to God, we are now free to love our fellows, be reconciled to them, and become a reconciling agent. Further, God pours his *agape* love into our hearts by the Holy Spirit (Rom. 5:5). In a very real sense, Christ loves through us, and the quality of this love is obviously much different from the *eros* love of the world. This agape kind of love is an interested love; it demonstrates an infinitely imaginative concern for the well-being of others. It continually, persistently meets needs. Further, it is not given because the object of love is loveable or fills a vacuum in the life of the lover. Rather, it is unconditional and given freely. Agape, seeking the best for the other, flows out regardless of the response, the character of the one loved, or the reaction of society. Agape is always vulnerable, open to suffering. In a word, agape love is reconciling. It

takes the initiative and heals, restores, and cures broken lives and relationships because of its complete selflessness. This is God's kind of love
and the kind of love demonstrated in Christ. And with Christ in one's
life, this reconciling love can be bestowed on others. If these truths are
not relevant to today's ruptured society, one wonders what is.

Finally, reconciled to God and others, we find reconciliation within
and we become free, really free, to function as mature members of society. Many tend to think of our sophisticated culture with its rejection of
the old superstitions and taboos of the past as one quite free from fear.
That which formerly bound the human personality has now been shown
up as false, we are told. We can grow and expand. True, we have laid to
rest much that should have been buried long ago, but though our cultural development and enlightenment have eliminated some of the old
manifestations of bondage, they have done little to solve the difficulty
of estrangement from one's true self. Multitudes still struggle with inner
bondage. As Paul put it in Romans, "I do not understand my own actions.
For I do not do what I want, but I do the very thing I hate. . . . I see in
my members another law at war with the law of my mind and making
me captive" (Rom. 7:15, 23 RSV).

But in Christ one is truly free, free from imprisonment to the corrupt
self. Life takes on new meaning. The questions of today's postmoderns—
Who am I? Where am I going?—are satisfyingly answered. People truly
can become an "authentic self." That is reconciliation, and that is most
applicable to today's bewildered world. Because God is concerned with
the whole person, the needs of the whole person are met in the Lord
Jesus Christ. That constitutes the Good News that we share.

There are other biblical terms and concepts concerning salvation that
space simply forbids considering, for example, propitiation, adoption,
new creation, and covenant. But perhaps the bare outline of these aspects
of redemption may enable us to begin developing such utter and complete confidence in the atonement of Jesus Christ that we shall herald
that gospel with a positive joy and enthusiasm. This ushers us into a
brief consideration of the importance of acquiring confidence in the
actual message we are to proclaim.

Confidence in the Power of the Gospel

Paul said, "I am not ashamed of the gospel, because it is the power
of God for the salvation of everyone who believes" (Rom. 1:16 NIV).
Such must be our spirit and attitude. The right approach was voiced

by C. H. Spurgeon when on a certain occasion a young ministerial student asked him how to defend the gospel successfully. Spurgeon replied, "How do you defend a lion? You don't. You just turn him loose." But is one justified in having such confidence in the gospel? The answer is an emphatic yes, because it is the Good News about God from God. Its source and its content are divine. The *kerygma* is the "sword of the Spirit" (Eph. 6:17) in all evangelism. This is why confidence in the power of the message is most reasonable and an important part of our theology of evangelism. Even though the postmodern's worldview rejects absolute truth, it still exists. And with a good apologetic approach, we can have confidence in the power of the gospel to communicate. This clearly implies that we need not rely on human ingenuity, psychological manipulations, dramatics, or any mere human invention to convince people of the truth and relevance of the message. God will speak for himself through his Word. The Holy Spirit will press home the truth (John 16:7–11).

Furthermore, the gospel speaks directly to the human situation as can no other truth. Whether or not people will admit their desperate need of reconciliation, it is actually everyone's deepest longing. The gospel always stands as the most relevant message anyone can hear. This point is clear, but right here we must be most careful. We must present the gospel to the living human situation. We must never simply grind out the truth, especially gospel truth, in a barrage of clichés. A cold delivery of evangelical orthodoxy rarely strikes home to the needy heart. Just delivering a message can in one sense be a "savour of death unto death" (2 Cor. 2:16 KJV). We must speak to real people in real human situations in love and Holy Spirit power. Their fears, frustrations, and thwarted ambitions have genuine substance. Their sin is real and concrete. They cry for help where they are. To the true witness, people matter. People matter as much as doctrinal principles. Our Lord's ministry reflected this, as he addressed people in their actual living situation. He talked about concrete, contemporary issues, never compromising principle, and always addressing people in their personal, immediate needs in the strength, wisdom, and power of the Spirit of God.

We who are evangelistically minded need to be conscious of this. Some of us are so concerned with orthodoxy, we forget that truth standing alone is irrelevant—if not an outright abstraction. Orthodoxy is important, but the orthodox gospel must be put in the terms of life itself and presented in love to real people. This God honors.

Suffice it to say that our message is one of power and relevance. It meets the deepest human needs, and we must have utter confidence in it if we are to be effective as the evangelistic church.

Colaborers with God

Another essential principle centers in a developing theology of evangelism as expressed by Paul to the Corinthian believers: "We are God's fellow workers" (1 Cor. 3:9 rsv). The rationale for this principle can be found in the truth previously mentioned that the mission to evangelize must be seen essentially as God's mission, the *missio Dei*. As the World Council of Churches has stated, "Mission is basically understood as God working out His purpose for His creation; the church does not have a separate mission of its own. It is called to participate in God's mission. The missionary call is a call for participation."[14]

God stands as the Evangelist, and we are merely colaborers in the sublime task. God essentially does the work. Jesus said, "Apart from me, you can do nothing" (John 15:5 niv). This must be kept constantly before the church. We can so easily get bogged down in the details of either our biblical and theological studies or the practical work of the church that we miss a central theme of the Scriptures. This is a truth we must never lose sight of. It will save us from a "sanctified humanism" that has so often plagued evangelism.

But as implied earlier, there is a parallel truth—perhaps a paradoxical truth—that God never redeems anyone apart from the instrumentality of his people, the church. This may seem an overstatement, yet the Scriptures bear it out. Pentecost's thousands came to Christ through the witness of Peter and the Twelve. Cornelius, though addressed by an angel, heard the gospel from Simon. Paul, who was actually accosted by the glorified Christ himself, heard what he was to do from Ananias. And though sent by an angel, it was still Philip who taught the Ethiopian eunuch about Christ. In commenting on this truth, R. C. H. Lenski points out, "Here we see how Jesus honors His ministry. Philip is sent to the eunuch by an angel; it is not the angel who is sent to teach the eunuch. And this is the case wherever the gospel is to be offered."[15] Through the New Testament and subsequent church history the principle persists.

The principle that we are colaborers with God involves two important implications relative to the church. First, we can be assured of success because God stands with us—or perhaps we should say that we stand with God. Of course, success cannot be judged by human standards. But if this is God's work in which we engage as colaborers, final success becomes certain. This should be a great encouragement and a strong stimulus to tireless effort. We are never alone.

Second, an awesome responsibility rests on the church. If God has no other basic plan for world redemption outside of the use of the agency of his whole people, the mandate to cooperate with God in the work becomes pressing indeed. Therefore, to kingdom progress we enthusi-astically thrust ourselves. Some time ago, while preaching on the neces-sity of Christians becoming witnesses for Christ, I was waxing a bit too eloquent, and I made the statement that unless God's people become enthusiastic witnesses, many will not be converted. After the service a young lady challenged me on my statement. She contended that those whom God has elected will be converted regardless of what we do. A strong element of truth can be found on that side of the paradoxical coin of election and freedom. But there is the other side of the salvation coin that declares that God uses his people in the quest for world evange-lization, and the implications of what will happen if God's people fail in the mission can be legitimately drawn. At least Ezekiel seemed to think so. He tells us:

> So you, son of man, I have made a watchman for the house of Israel; when-ever you hear a word from my mouth, you shall give them warning from me. If I say to the wicked, O wicked man, you shall surely die, and you do not speak to warn the wicked to turn from his way, that wicked man shall die in his iniquity, but his blood I will require at your hand. But if you warn the wicked to turn from his way, and he does not turn from his way; he shall die in his iniquity, but you will have saved your life.

Ezekiel 33:7–9 RSV

My interview with the young lady was somewhat reminiscent of William Carey's encounter with the old brother who told him to sit down after his plea for missionaries, for if God wanted to convert the heathen, he would do it without Carey's help. We are thankful today that Carey did not sit down but zealously went after men and women for Christ. Such must be the attitude of the contemporary church if we take seri-ously the principle of being colaborers with God. This seems vital for a sound theology of evangelism. The local church as a whole must be moti-vated to engage in mission, and it will not happen unless God's people get rooted in a sound understanding of the *missio Dei*. In that arena of labor, God uses wise methodologies.

Basic Biblical Principles of Evangelistic Methodology

The theme of evangelistic methodology could become all but an end-less volume in itself. Yet it is vital to see, if only in simplest form, some of these important biblical principles, because evangelistic activity that neglects or ignores scriptural methodologies is doomed to weakness, if not failure. Tersely put, we must do God's work in God's way. Looking first into the ministry of our Lord, we can identify ten salient points that should inform our methodology.

1. Primarily, Jesus unreservedly gave of himself; he shared his own personhood on behalf of the needy. He did this in a fashion and depth we never can, yet we must emulate the principle if we are to be effective as "evangelists." This stands as foundational.

2. Jesus confronted people with the great issues. He was never sidetracked on theological fads. He kept on the main line. Yet he confronted these profound truths with a marvelous simplicity. "The common people heard him gladly" (Mark 12:37 KJV). The communicator who overshoots the people is not following Jesus' example.

3. Our Lord never compromised the demanding claims of the gospel to win followers. He always presented his absolute lordship as the cost of discipleship. As we see in the classic case of the rich young ruler, Jesus never cut corners to win anyone.

4. At the same time, Christ had profound respect for human personality. He never bulldozed anyone. He was always patient, understanding, and loving. With dignity—and that in a good, mature sense—he never made anyone feel like less of a person, even in his occasional scathing denunciations.

5. He presented the truth uncompromisingly and challenged people to decide then and there. He asked Simon, Andrew, James, and John to choose right then between their nets and discipleship (Mark 1:16–20). Matthew was directly and pointedly confronted with the life-deciding issue of whether it would be God or money. And he had to decide while he sat right at the tax-collector's bench that was loaded with money. A principle emerges here that many need to grasp today. So often we leave people to think over the gospel, robbing it of its challenge to immediate commitment. There is the time to wait, to be sure, but there is also the time to call for decision.

6. It seems evident from the life of our Lord that he had a definite strategy. For example, "his face was set toward Jerusalem" (Luke 9:53 RSV). Jesus knew what he was about and where he was going. To update this principle into modern terms, Christ had a "program." He had a "statement of purpose" that he followed. This too the church needs to learn. Churches are to be purpose driven.

7. Jesus did not attempt to do all the work himself. He taught, encouraged, nurtured, and commissioned disciples. The implications of this fact are clear and numerous as regards the local church.

8. Above all Jesus was compassionate. He saw the people as sheep without a shepherd. No personal sacrifice was ever too great to hinder the Lord's ministry. He was always in the spirit of the towel and basin, washing feet. For he said, "The Son of man did not come to be served, but to serve, and to give His life" (Matt. 20:28).
9. Jesus ministered to the whole person. Physical, mental, and spiritual needs were met quite indiscriminately. Whatever or wherever needs arose, he met them. He knew little of the so-called divisions of secular and sacred, spiritual and physical, or saving and social gospel.
10. Lastly, Christ saw prayer as the one indispensable exercise in his mission. How can it be otherwise with us?

Thus our Lord ministered the Good News, and people came by the multitudes to see and hear, and not a few believed.

Pentecost Principles

Let us take a final look at Pentecost. It provides something of a model for local church evangelism. Granted, much more than evangelistic principles are implied by the day of Pentecost; that day was a singular epoch in the church. Still, much can be learned concerning local mission from the events of the day, provided we attempt to learn without doing violence to the other great theological truths of Pentecost.

First of all, Pentecost is telling us that the age of the Spirit has dawned. God has not withdrawn from salvation history with the ascension of Jesus Christ; the converse is true. Jesus is now in the work as profoundly as in the days of his flesh. All effective mission is carried on in the context of a Spirit-led, inspired, and energized ministry.

Pentecost also points up the fact that before anything significant happens in the unbelieving community, something of profound significance must happen to the church. The city of Jerusalem took little note of the 120 followers of the Nazarene gathered for ten days in an upper room. But when the disciples were deeply moved by God, the multitude came together. And they were "confounded," "amazed," and "perplexed" until they finally gave up trying to discover a rationale for the phenomenon and asked, "What does this mean?" It was then, and not until then, that Peter could stand up and say, "This is that!" and present the gospel of Christ.

This is always the ideal context of great evangelism. The outside world becomes so perplexed by the wonder of what God has done and is doing in and through his church that they begin asking questions. In this sort of setting, the gospel can be effectively communicated. Surely all of us should earnestly pray for such a move of God's Spirit on his church.

Of prime importance, on the day of Pentecost, Christ was preached. The disciples had but one message. This does not mean that later the New Testament church failed to minister in many different ways and to preach many other truths. They were not afraid of the social implications of the gospel, for example. It surely does not mean they failed to confront men and women in their own life situation and approach them with that particular aspect of the Good News that was most appealing and relevant. But whether we see Stephen addressing the biblically oriented Sanhedrin, Peter appealing to the God-fearing Gentile Cornelius, or Paul preaching to the philosophical sophisticates of Athens, to each audience they simply presented Christ as the answer to life's basic needs. This is an inescapable principle of effective evangelistic endeavor and a vital part of a sound theology of evangelism.

As this chapter comes to a close, recognize that this mere skeleton of a theology of evangelism needs much meat hung on the bare bones. But if the Spirit can breathe on us, hopefully these bones can live. With this framework of theology, let us move on to consider the more practical aspects and problems of evangelism in reaching our postmodern generation. There is a job to do and obstacles to overcome.

Questions and Issues for Study

1. Why does theology have an important place in evangelism, especially for postmoderns?
2. How does one overcome the reluctance to get into theology?
3. Where can we get the theology we need?
4. What is the theology of God in regard to the evangelistic mission?
5. What is the theology of Jesus Christ?
6. What is the theology of the Holy Spirit?
7. What is the theology of salvation?
8. What is the theology of judgment?
9. What role does the church play in deepening its members' theological grasp of the Christian faith?
10. What are you doing to increase your knowledge and understanding of God, and does it have a part in evangelism?

seven

Obstacles to Overcome

Why do some churches seemingly have little success in reaching people, particularly postmoderns, for Christ? Granted, these young people constitute a new phenomenon in society, but surely the gospel can be made appealing to them as to any societal group. Why are we losing them? Could it simply be that the contemporary church has failed to address this different worldview relevantly? That is to say, have we failed to communicate the gospel in a fashion that makes the "grand old story" fresh and attractive to this new mind-set?

We have mentioned this problem several times already, especially on a more individualistic basis, especially in the chapter on apologetics. Now it seems appropriate to attack the issue and deal with the problem on a churchwide level. This we must do if we are to see large numbers of postmoderns effectively evangelized. Of course, there are other obstacles to be dealt with, but relevant communication of the whole church seems the highest hurdle to clear, so we begin there.

The Postmodern Problem of Communication

Despite the complexity of the issue, the obstacle that communication presents to mission can be described quite simply as the need of the church to get on the communicative wavelength of this new segment of society. In light of the fact that by and large postmoderns ignore the church and are ignorant of the church's communication motif, how do we get the ear of this urbanized, existentially oriented society?

We may ask, Why should the quandary of communication be such a stinging issue today? Do we not have means of communication at our disposal that the church has never had before? We have the Internet, TV, and many other means of mass communication. What has precipitated the situation? The problems may appear to be only those of language, vocabulary, failure to use modern terminology, and the like. These can be problems, but they are quite secondary. The basic difficulty is essentially philosophical and sociological. In recent years the very fabric of society itself has been so altered that the fundamental nature of Western understandings of truth, reality, meaning, and social structures makes communicating to this new mind-set extremely difficult. Perhaps a cursory survey of the past few centuries will help us see this in bold relief.

A Review of the Past

For millennia people lived in something of a tribal context. The members of the tribe fished, hunted, farmed, and relaxed together. Each individual truly belonged to the group. Society was structured around a close-knit community that wove into its fabric the value systems inherited from the past. This community-type lifestyle provided a very viable, stable society. With this kind of social structure, communication was no problem. As a matter of fact, a tribal person could scarcely breathe without the whole community knowing and discussing it. Communication was a societal enterprise. It was a shared life with shared ideas, experiences, and above all, shared truth and values. This lifestyle was epitomized in the feudal system and, more recently, in the American interdependent frontier.

But approximately five hundred years ago—a very recent time in the light of human history—a crack in the community dike appeared. The printing press burst on the scene. The coming of the printed book began to change radically the entire structure of how the average person received information and knowledge, hence, his or her value system. Before Gutenberg, only the elect few could have a library. The printing press made books available to all. Now everyone could read, at least potentially. And how does one normally read a book? Alone! Hence, the printing press provided the beginnings of the modern rise of individualism. The steps toward an individualistic "atomic" society began.

Furthermore, the Renaissance and Enlightenment broke in on the scene almost simultaneously. Rationalism, empiricism, and materialism all gained ascendancy in people's system of values, influencing the way they gain truth and make value judgments. With a rugged individualism, modern man was born.

Then the industrial revolution began to break on the horizon in the Western world. This was more than a mere crack in the dike, a veritable tidal wave of social change swept across society and all but drowned community life as it had been known for ages.

Invention followed invention. Factories mushroomed to produce the fruits of the revolution. People moved by the millions from their old, close-knit communities to the rapidly growing urban industrial areas. The new residential areas into which they moved were so diverse that their neighbors were not necessarily their fellow workers and perhaps not even acquaintances. To this were added long working hours and/or time-consuming travel. As the revolution continued, isolation deepened until, as Gavin Reid states, "men have in fact become non-community animals."[1] And along with mushrooming materialism, they have become very worldly "animals."

One further step was needed, however, to complete the revolution and breakdown of community life. Many people still met in groups outside the workshop, for example, in clubs, hobby groups, and the church. Then the technical revolution dawned and the final step was taken. Television, radio, the Internet, and other mass media put amusement and communication right into each home. A person no longer needs his or her social group. Leisure time can now be spent inside the four walls of one's own castle—the home. And with this isolation, the inherited value systems, the concepts of how truth and reality are discerned, totter on the brink of rapid change.

Actually a real rebellion is in the making. Modern, and especially postmodern, people, sensing a lack of fulfillment, broke the restraints of the old community to "do their own thing." The fact that in America and Western Europe some 90 percent of the population live in urbanized industrialized areas means that a sense of community has been virtually obliterated. Consequently the church must face the fact that community, with the restraints it fostered and the teaching that has been known for millennia, has all but passed away. This sociological phenomenon has precipitated a real problem for the church. What are the results?

The church is in a quandary. As Reid points out, "[The current state of our society] shows . . . that we do not start with the advantages of the Old Testament prophet or of a New Testament apostle or even of a John Wesley. One thing was common to them all—they spoke to real communities and to community-man."[2] Today the urbanized church is not talking to people in community with the same worldview and system of values and truth of past years. It appears many Christians in the church have not truly realized this fact and have not addressed the issue seriously. It would seem our churches are often still relating to people as if they were yet living in community with a system of values that has held sway for countless generations. Hence, a ghetto mentality takes over, and postmoderns are left outside.

We must awaken to the seriousness of this issue. The greatest threat to the gospel today in Western postmodern society is not impurity of doctrine or worldly compromise; rather, it is this problem of communication to those "outside" the church. Unless Christians can gain the ear of postmodern, noncommunity people, then not only are these individuals in desperate spiritual plight, but the future of the church is in trouble.

Therefore it would seem quite clear that the old way of doing church that depended on speaking to people in community as they gathered in our church buildings, and teaching them on the basis of the epistemology of the past is over as far as effectiveness is concerned. In a word, the church must overhaul—sometimes radically overhaul—many of its approaches.

Some Suggested Solutions

The problem for the church is obviously complex and deep-seated. But perhaps the picture is not quite as dark as it may at first appear. There is one thing the church can do that would be of genuine significance. If the breakdown of community and a changing worldview have precipitated the church's failure to attract postmoderns, can the church recreate community and come to understand postmodernism, getting on their communicative and social level? People still relate, and there is an innate dynamic that makes us all—regardless of our particular worldview—desire a relationship with our own kind, not with the computer or TV, whether we realize it or not. Postmoderns are by and large sensitive to this need. We cannot turn back the sociological clock, but why not build small communities through the lives of understanding church members? If members of the church could be enlightened to see that people long for meaningful involvement with others despite technological substitutes, then they could be equipped to build community around postmoderns. This would provide a tremendous milieu for communicating the gospel.

Of course we must never compromise the truth of God's Word, as stressed earlier. We must just get it over to postmoderns in a way to which they can relate. Is not this the principle behind the house group, personal evangelism, relational evangelism, youth Bible study groups, and so on? This is especially true to relational evangelism. Church members need to be trained to establish personal relationships so as to share Christ. In principle, these approaches could at least be a beginning and a relevant way to approach the evangelistic ministry in the local church. Of course such an approach will mean that the church cannot rely solely on what is done within the four walls of its buildings. Moreover, it means in this area of ministry the church must equip Christians for the task, just as, in an earlier chapter, I contended that believers must be equipped in apologetics.

In summary, the breakdown in community and the loss of older community values has precipitated a new worldview and resulting communication problems that hopefully can begin to be met by a new community through which Christ can be proclaimed. May the church be prophetic and prepare for what lies ahead and not get entangled with old, irrelevant methodologies, lest we lose the ear of the postmoderns all together. We must not let that happen.

Creating Practical Answers

Now how can all this be done? Space again precludes a detailed presentation; an outline must suffice. Here are some suggested approaches:

- Instruct workers on the nature and philosophy of postmodernism: how this new generation sees life, its values, the way objective truth and reality are encountered, and the like. In a word, help the church understand this generation.
- Make leaders aware of the importance of apologetics and get them informed and involved in how to use a good argument.
- Be certain those involved have a clear-cut grasp of the full gospel of Jesus Christ (Rom. 1:16).
- Create structures of community wherein postmoderns will develop a sense of belonging and feel at home. Peer support and love can prevail. Help believers to establish personal relationships.

- Be willing to change. A new day has dawned; old programs may have to go.
- Pray much. These new-generation people truly need Christ. The church cannot let them slip through our fingers.
- Trust God to lead, give wisdom, and empower for the task.

More along these lines will be presented in the next chapter.

A Secondary Problem

It may be helpful before moving on to other issues to look briefly at the secondary problem of communications mentioned earlier; that is the problem of language. The criticisms are quite valid that inward-looking, traditional churches have developed something of an "in-language." Such a vocabulary sounds strange, if not unintelligible, to the postmodern ear. It may well be true that the "language of Zion" once communicated to people, but that is certainly not the case today, especially to the younger generations. In reality we are back to square one with the problem of the first-century church. They had to learn to use a common idiom to convey their message. So must we.

To update our religious language is not easy, however. Old speech patterns and emotive words do not change easily. Nonetheless, the church must attempt to proclaim the good news of Christ in a vocabulary that is understandable to the postmodern generation. True, we have many good theological words that are very descriptive. Moreover, a certain amount of technical terminology is inescapable in any field, as we see in the scientific world. Thus the best course seems to be to use as simple a vocabulary as possible; then, when a more technical term must be employed that we think people will not grasp, we should take ample time to define, explain, and illustrate its meaning in words and pictures that can be understood. Word pictures communicate today. The "story" approach is a very viable tool. This is what the apostles and early preachers did with the Koine Greek. Jesus told stories, which we call parables. We must work at it. We are in the communication business, and if we fail to present the message in an understandable manner, we fail the gospel.

The point is that the churches must become conscious of these problems and diligently work on them. For example, some time back I had the opportunity to conduct a series of evangelistic services in Prague. There were attendees who were completely outside the church, living in a radically different framework of society. Furthermore, the translator was not fluent in English. Thus I had an external circumstance thrust on me that forced me to take a quite simple approach in my preaching. I had to be very careful in the choice of many words, but by keeping in mind the centrality of communicating Christ and working with a simple vocabulary, explaining words, attempting to understand the hearers' level, the message got over to the people. Now if we can see ourselves in a somewhat comparable situation with the postmodern that lives down the street, we should be able to declare Christ intelligibly.

Of course another aspect of the problem of communication that needs serious attention centers in what the hearers accept as the source and meaning of truth. In chapter 1 I briefly discussed the issue. There I attempted to point out that the spirit of relativism, a rejection of a purely rational-empirical epistemology, and the loss of absolutes prevail in the thinking of postmoderns. For them, truth is relative and "experience" rules. This way of thinking has to some extent influenced all of the younger generation. Subjectivism and existentialism are the criteria of truth for most. Dogmatic pronouncements are frowned on, especially when they come from those over thirty or forty. Consequently, spiritual concepts, although many people are quite interested in them, are up for grabs. If we are not aware of this climate and move to meet it, many will reject our message, which is by its very nature positive and spiritual and at times above mere rationalism. Let's get on their experience level as well as on a purely intellectual plane. That should appeal to them. But those issues have been amply emphasized.

After all is said and done, the Spirit of God is the one who convicts, convinces, and converts the unbeliever. As we positively present the kerygma without any dilution or shame, in a communicative framework, God will honor it. Moreover, it is often a moral problem more than an intellectual one that keeps people from Christ (John 3:20–21). Honest intellectual difficulties can normally be met by the sincere and knowledgeable Christian.

The Importance of Dialogue

The day also calls for a fresh look at the relevance of dialogue in communicating our faith. In Reuel L. Howe's significant work, *The Miracle of Dialogue,* he makes the point that dialogue is more than a mere method of communication, it is communication itself.[3] It can develop in-depth relationships, which are vital to sharing one's faith. The wise individual witness and the whole church body will see that this principle plays a major role in life, service, and ministry.

God's people need to understand the principles of dialogue. This really lies at the heart of what we call personal, relational evangelism. If Christians do not relate in depth to people, how can they win the unbeliever? Furthermore, church life itself should be structured in such a way as to allow for this type of interplay. Young people, who are moving away from a "come, sit, and listen" mentality, want to be heard. Dialogue is vital. No longer can we ignore this growing sentiment if we want to communicate to today's world.

In the final place, concerning the problems of communication, the wise witness will use all the modern means at his or her disposal. As much as one can move into mass media, radio, television, and drama, it should be done.

As fundamental and complex as the communication dilemma is, another serious issue arises that the church currently faces in its attempt to evangelize. We dare not forget the "social action" approach to ministry. We need to give a moment of attention to this obstacle to overcome.

The Problem of Social Action versus "Frontier Pietism"

The old conflict between what was once known as the "social gospel" and the pure and simple evangelism of "frontier pietism," as some have called it, is thankfully passing away. Let it be understood that God stands for the good of all mankind. He is that kind of God. And if God involves himself in the sociological milieu and needs of people, so must the church. God's people have no option. We need to do all we can to better the lot of our fellows, working for all people regardless of who they are or what their need. Only in that way can we be faithful to our Christian calling. As John Stott has said, "A hungry man has no ears." Why be polarized by a "social" or a "saving" ministry? The church can give itself to both social action and individual conversion; both are demanded in Scripture. Therefore, if people are hungry, we feed; if sick, we heal; if oppressed, we unite to free. Moreover, we live in such a social structure at the moment that, if we are to help the contemporary victim who "falls among thieves" on today's Jericho road, the church will probably have to form an action group and call itself the committee to make the Jericho road a safe freeway. But by the same token, if one's neighbor is individually lost without Christ, that need must also be met by confronting the lost with the good news of Christ in every way possible.

There really is no difficulty keeping this relationship between declaring the gospel and social action. We just find people where they are and whatever the need may be—social, physical, mental, or spiritual—in the name of Christ the church steps in to meet that need. As James Leo Garrett has well said, "The crux of the present argument is that both evangelism and social involvement are essential to the mission and obedience of Christians today . . . the 'both/and' stance is to be taken rather than either of the 'either/or' stances."[4] Hopefully this is not oversimplifying the issue. In principle, it is that straightforward, and perhaps some have made more of a problem of it than is warranted. A well-rounded New Testament theology can surely motivate the church to minister in God's purpose, which means finding people in the multitude of their perplexities and in the name of Christ meeting needs. That's what Jesus himself did. Those who know the Bible and church history understand how deeply involved the church has been in social action. For two millennia the great social movements have grown out of holistic evangelism.

When the postmodern world witnesses genuine concern for the total needs of people, they are attracted. Many social ministries can and should be undertaken by churches. As a concrete illustration, Daniel Blair has constructed a very viable and workable program for meeting the spiritual and social needs of the hearing impaired. It speaks of Christ's concern and meets a true need (see appendix A). We simply "find hurts and heal them."

But we must now move to consider an impediment to evangelism that is perhaps at least more keenly felt by the average church than any other obstacle.

The Problem of the Apathetic Church

A description of this obstacle to effective evangelism is not needed. We know it only too well. Many church members seem all but totally apathetic to the evangelistic challenge. Will the church ever awake to its responsibility? It has been stated that 90 percent of church members never once in their lifetime share their faith. There are probably several reasons for this spirit of lethargy and lack of concern. Often, the lack of genuine worship with its vitalizing influences can be blamed. Further, failure to root Christians in a knowledge of the Scriptures has no doubt contributed to a lackadaisical attitude toward the things of God. A dearth of dynamic leadership training also has probably been a negative influence in some places. Then, some churches take a theological stand for minimizing evangelism. Regardless of these and many other possible reasons, one thing is certain, the spirit of unconcern that has settled on many congregations is profoundly serious. All congregations battle this problem, at least to some extent.

What can be done to effect a spiritual awakening so that the fires of evangelism can burn brightly? In principle, the answer can be found in the fact that evangelism is really the overflow of a spiritually dynamic church. Rick Warren, pastor of the great Saddleback Community Church in California, declares in his well-received book *The Purpose Driven Church* that the spiritually healthy congregation is the one that evangelizes effectively and grows.[5] If we agree with this statement, then we must ask, How does a church become spiritually alive and healthy? If we are ever to attract the postmoderns—and people of every generation—we must have strong, spiritually alive churches.

In answer to this foundational question, it must be said at the outset that God's work through the Holy Spirit alone creates the spiritual dynamic sorely needed. To attack such a large theme in a few words again seems almost presumptuous. But if we can learn what God desires to accomplish among us, it may at least constitute a beginning.

In the first place, God has promised to bless and use the communication of his Word. Our Lord works in and through the sharing of biblical truth. But that teaching and preaching process must have certain ingredients. It must be prophetic; that is, the Word of God must be positively and forthrightly declared with a relevance to human needs as found today. We hear much emphasis on prophetic preaching, and rightly so, for "thus says the Lord" is what people desperately need to understand. But the pastor must communicate the message with a relevant challenge to relevant needs. And all the teachers and witnesses of the congregation must do likewise. A real part of this centers in motivating people to action. The spirit of challenge becomes important. This does not necessarily mean a hard-sell approach, but we are to preach, teach, and share Scripture so as to move people to Christ. Jesus asked for decisions. The church needs that element of exhortation. As James tells us, we are not to be mere hearers of the Word, but also doers (James 1:22). The preacher and teacher must always communicate the message with that principle and goal in mind. Good exposition of the Scriptures and the biblical challenge are central. It appears that one hears little expository preaching anymore. Preachers and pastors are to take seriously the call to "preach the word" (2 Tim. 4:2 RSV).

Further, the problem of apathy can be somewhat mitigated by attempting to correct those areas previously mentioned as some of the causes for it. The church should strive to revitalize worship and keep the purpose and role of the church before the people. Training the leadership also helps tremendously. All must work toward making the local church a real "body of Christ." And as already stressed, all that is done to get Christians rooted and grounded in the Scriptures creates a great step forward.

But in the final analysis, God's people must rely basically on prayer and faith. If our churches are lethargic about the evangelistic task and in need of awakening, let us pray and trust God to revive his work in the midst of years (Hab. 3:2). The church desperately needs this commitment, and spiritual awakening comes essentially through prayer. Moreover, leaders in the church need to pray first for themselves that the quickening may begin in them. Then the spirit of prayer will spread. It may be only one or two at the start, but God can fan the fire and a conflagration will erupt. Oftentimes it is a mistake to attempt to involve the whole church in everything. It may be a very small praying remnant through whom God will send his blessings. May we work and pray for all that God has and trust him to open up many other lives as well. The epilogue deals with this issue in more depth.

For meeting such a pressing issue as apathy, these suggestions do not seem exhaustive. We can be encouraged by the multiplying signs, which indicate that God is at work in marvelous ways among his people, encouraging them in prayer. Renewal may be on its way.

We now move to the final problem to be discussed.

The Problem of Conserving the Results

Every pastor has experienced the disappointment of seeing a person make a profession of faith, carry on for a time, and then seemingly fall away. How can we conserve the results of evangelistic endeavors? A few simple guidelines may help eliminate this all-too-common problem.

Initially, there must be a proper presentation of the gospel itself. That goes without saying. The church must be careful to avoid ministering in such a way that new converts stand in human wisdom rather than in the power of God (1 Cor. 2:5). But given that, a proper philosophy of new member orientation on how to be a maturing Christian is essential. Often more effort is spent on integrating new believers into the structures of the local church than into the basics of spiritual growth. As important for Christian maturity as the local church may be, the prime need of the new convert centers in learning the great disciplines and doctrines of the Christian experience. Primarily God wants his people to abide in Christ (John 15:4). Church commitment will then follow.

At least seven points should form the foundation of new-Christian orientation:

1. A rooting and grounding in the salvation experience. The new convert must know he or she rests securely in Christ. Without this conviction, Christian maturity stagnates (Heb. 6:1–8).

2. An overall grasp of the great doctrines of the faith. Such an orientation stands essential for one's understanding of all that transpires in the developing Christian experience (Eph. 3:17–19).
3. An understanding of what the Bible is and how to read it profitably. The new baby in Christ is to "long for the pure milk of the word" that he or she may grow thereby (1 Peter 2:2).
4. A basic primer on prayer. If one is to be strong in Christ, one must learn how to pray (Eph. 6:18).
5. A grasp of how to achieve victory in trials, temptations, and testings. In Christ there is victory, and the new Christian must learn how to be an overcomer (Rom. 8:37).
6. An understanding of the meaning and place of the local church in one's life. The new believer must feel that he or she is an essential part of the church (Heb. 10:24–25).
7. A grasp of the necessity of witnessing and service. The new Christian needs to understand how to begin a life of witness and service for Christ (Acts 1:8).

If a new convert and church member gets established in these seven areas, he or she surely stands a far better chance of carrying on in the Christian life. These points actually delineate the principle of abiding in Christ, and where there are spiritually healthy believers, there will be a spiritually healthy church. If proper materials to teach the above principles are unobtainable, let the pastor and leaders write and produce their own. But today a multitude of helps can usually be found.

Another profitable program that many churches have used with success is the assignment of "shepherds" to the new members. Let one or more members be responsible for the nurture, care, and guarding of the young "sheep." Obviously these so-called shepherds or mentors must be mature believers themselves, and they will need to be trained for the task. Some administration for such a program is also called for, but the results are well worth the time and effort.

Finally, pastors must do all in their power to be guardians of the whole flock, particularly the new members. The imaginative pastor can find myriad ways to help the new convert grow in his or her faith.

Conclusion

There are problems that impede evangelism to be sure, many not even touched on here. But the leader and Christian worker must remember that no problem surfaces that is greater than God. If God is in this mission enterprise—and he surely is—solutions and success can be found. The church has fabulous resources for being the victor in the battle.

Questions and Issues for Study

1. What are the essential obstacles to overcome in evangelizing postmoderns?
2. How can you address the problem of communication?
3. How can you address the problem of human sin?
4. How can you address the problem of alienation from God?
5. How can you address the problem of loneliness by relational evangelism?
6. How can you address the problem of a "meaningless" life?
7. How can you make the gospel make sense?
8. How important is it for a person to make a real commitment to Christ?
9. How do you address the problem of peer pressure to reject the gospel?
10. Where do you get the strength and wisdom to be an effective communicator for Christ?

eight

Equipping God's People for the Task

The burden of the preceding pages has been an attempt to present the obligations of the whole church in developing evangelistic outreach to the revolutionary generation. The New Age mind-set demands a new commitment of all Christians. Most genuine believers are reasonably knowledgeable of their responsibility to mission, grasping, at least in some measure, the implications of Christ's Great Commission. One would further suppose that a reasonable percentage has developed something of an understanding of the evangelistic task and experienced some motivation to engage in the grand enterprise. However, we must ask the question, Do God's people really know *how* to evangelize today? At times there seems to be a spirit of frustration as evangelistically minded believers seek ways and means of implementing their convictions. We have never lived in a psychological, sociological, and philosophical atmosphere comparable to today's revolutionary spirit. Moreover, as stressed earlier, the old forms to which many congregations are shackled rarely suffice to communicate the Good News to the mass of contemporary New Agers. What can be done? Can an effective strategy for outreach be found that will work today? Yes! The solution can be found in a principle as old as the Scriptures themselves. It could be called "back to the future"—back to the Bible to discover future effective ministry. The key to relevant mission in this or any generation always rests essentially in the New Testament concept of the *ministry of the laity.*

Lay-Centered Ministry

It can be stated right at the outset that unless the church recaptures and implements the scriptural principle of a lay-centered ministry, little hope exists for fulfilling the commission to evangelize our post-modern day. It hardly seems necessary to present any kind of apologetic for the principle of a lay-centered ministry; the Bible abounds with the principle, of which most are aware, as Michael Green tells us:

> Christianity was from its inception a lay movement, and so it continued for a remarkably long time. Ministry for the early Christians was a happy, "unselfconscious effort." They went about quite naturally sharing their faith, gossiping the gospel, as it were. They were zealous, enthusiastic; they could not help but speak of the things they had experienced. They were not "professionals," they were unpaid. As a consequence, they were taken seriously—especially was this true among the lower classes—and the movement spread. . . . All of this makes it abundantly clear that in contrast to the present day, when Christianity is highly intellectualized and dispensed by a professional clergy to a constituency increasingly confined to the middle classes, in the early days the faith was spontaneously spread by informal evangelists.[1]

Simply put, through the ministry of first-century laypeople, the masses of that generation were effectively reached for Christ. Those early believers understood their generation and impacted it tremendously. Thus it can be concluded that in the early church there was little if any distinction between full-time ministers and the so-called laity, at least in the sense of responsibility to spread the Good News. Every Christian became an evangelist. They well understood the principle, as George Goyder, a layman himself, has graphically put it, that there are to be "no passengers in the church. All are called."[2]

Regrettably, in subsequent years of church history, a high clericalism began to develop. More and more, as the clergy assumed command of the evangelistic mission, the average layperson was slowly squeezed out or opted out. The clergy began to dominate the entire life of the church. Through the centuries, this attitude hardened until in the course of time the English word *lay* became a synonym for *amateur* as over against *professional*, or *unqualified* as opposed to *expert*. How often we hear, "I'm just a layperson." This can usually be taken as an apology for not being able to do evangelism very well. Of course, some church members have not objected to this development. More than a few have acquired a sort of "spectator mentality," and what the average member seems to want, as Sir John Lawrence put it, is "a building which looks like a church; a clergyman dressed in a way he approves; services of the kind he's been used to, and to be left alone."[3] Such an attitude exhibits little if any real interest in evangelism, let alone engaging enthusiastically in the task.

On the other hand, there have been reactions through the years to the clericalism of the church. Some have been strong; hence, movements arose like the Quakers and Plymouth Brethren who have virtually rejected the idea of a professional clergy altogether. Other reactions have not been quite as cavalier. However, the bulk of Christians seem to accept some sort of dualism between ministers and laypeople but have no real grasp of the respective roles they play in the missions of the church. Yet a strict dualism of this sort is never satisfying and becomes a constant source of inefficiency if not irritation. Can such a situation find a resolution? Hopefully, yes, because evangelizing the postmodern age depends on it. This new generation reacts positively to genuine spirituality and loving concern. Thus the whole people of God must exemplify these qualities in Christ's service as they relate to the needy world on a personal level. Person-to-person encounter constitutes the key to reaching postmoderns and thus demands commitment from the whole church. This fulfills the biblical concept of the church as the ministering body of Christ.

There are many metaphors found in the New Testament to describe the people of God. The Scriptures present the figures of the church as the bride of Christ, God's vineyard, God's flock, the Father's family, God's building, a holy priesthood, the new Israel, and a holy nation. One of the most graphic, and that which seemed to be a favorite of Paul's, views the church as the *body of Christ*. This metaphor has two important implications relative to Christian service. First, as the human body has different parts with different functions, so does the church. To say all members in a church are to do the same thing in ministry is quite inappropriate. Abilities and gifts vary widely with each member, just as in the human physical body. That is why Paul asks rhetorically:

All are not apostles, are they? All are not prophets, are they? All are not
teachers, are they? All are not workers of miracles, are they? All do not
have gifts of healing, do they? All do not speak with tongues, do they? All
do not interpret, do they? . . . For even as the body is one and yet has many
members, and all the members of the body, though they are many, are
one body, so also is Christ. For by one Spirit we were all baptized into one
body, whether Jews or Greeks, whether slaves or free, and we were all
made to drink of one Spirit.

1 Corinthians 12:29–30, 12–13

God has made up the church with a diversity of members and
corresponding functions. That basic reality must be recognized. It has
much to do with evangelism, as shall be shown.

In the second place, the figure of the church as a body suggests that
in the congregation's diversity there still remains a central, inescapable
unity. The body is "one." All the members stand equal and one before
God. All are "in Christ." The one and same Spirit enables every Christian to say, "Jesus is Lord." Moreover, as continually stressed, the commission to evangelize is given to the entire body. John Stott reminds us
that "the essential unity of the Church, originating in the call of God
and illustrated in the metaphors of Scripture, leads us to this conclusion: The responsibilities, which God has entrusted to His Church, He
has entrusted to His whole Church."[4] Herein rests the dilemma of clericalism, anticlericalism, and an unsatisfying, unbiblical dualism. But a
clear grasp of the unity in diversity of the body can save us from all three
errors. The church as a diversified yet unified body fulfills its purpose
in worship and ministry. Thus the dilemma finds its resolution.

What relationship then is implied between the so-called laity and
clergy in the body figure? The first fact to realize centers in the concept
that the laity are the whole people of God and the clergy have received
the privilege of oversight, shepherding, and equipping the entire body
for service. A figure may be helpful here to show the proper relationship. Elton Trueblood likens the clergyman to the coach of a football
team. The coach instructs, teaches, motivates, and helps direct the play,
but the team (the laity) assumes the major role in actually playing the
game. At the same time, however, the so-called minister is a Christian
as well. By virtue of that fact he or she also "plays the game," the minister becomes a playing coach, as it were. This is essentially true because
he or she is a Christian, not simply clergy. Remember, the term *lay* means
"people"—all the people of God. As Stott has told us, "if anybody belongs
to anybody in the church, it is not the laity who belongs to the clergy,
but the clergy who belongs to the laity."[5] With this relationship in the
diversified but integrated body, the work can go forward effectively. In

most congregations, instruction in these principles is still needed, although much has been written about these concepts.

The Place of Christian Education in Outreach

It seems correct to say that, if God's people can grasp their role in mission, that is to say, if the principles set forth are taken seriously and implemented, something of a revolution could well take place in most congregations. But to move the layperson out of his or her comfortable pew and into the arena of evangelism constitutes no small undertaking. Years of relative inactivity on the part of the average church member will not be easily changed. It will take motivation. The Holy Spirit, the great Motivator, always works on the basis of truth, the truth of God's Word. Thus grounding and educating the church in the Scriptures, particularly in the area of the Christian mission and the overall responsibility of the whole people of God in the task, is where to begin. And it does seem reasonably safe to assume there are a number of members in the local church who will respond to the call of service and evangelism when they come to understand the mandate of the Bible. God's people must get grounded in the Word, and, in some measure, that task rests on the church leadership.

The next demanding task in the educational process will be to equip God's people for their ministry. The Lambeth Conference in Britain made the following appeal: "No one wants untrained troops. . . . We need a Christian education explosion comparable to that in the secular world." Then it was declared, "The Conference believes that there is an urgent need for increase in the quantity and quality of training available for laypeople for their task in the world."[6] It seems quite apt to conclude that such Christian education in depth stands as perhaps one of the most pressing needs in our churches today, that is if we hope to evangelize effectively our generation. Of course, the term *Christian education* conveys a very broad, inclusive concept. It implies nothing less than equipping the entire company of the saints for the work of the ministry, as Paul told us (Eph. 4:12). That is no mean task.

When launching a churchwide educational program, several elements should be recognized as essential in developing an adequate structure of ministry. First, a valid and comprehensive objective is called for. A church needs a well-defined statement of purpose in its educational pursuits. The effective church is the purpose-driven church. Roger L. Shinn gives the three objectives of Christian education based on Mark 12:29–31: (1) to grow in relation to God, (2) to develop trustful and responsible relations with others, and (3) to become a whole person.[7] Without some such basic, purposeful goal for education, few Christians will ever become challenged and equipped to engage successfully in evangelistic outreach, or any phase of Christian service for that matter.

Second, the content of Christian education should be as comprehensive as God's entire redemptive purpose for the world. Revealed kingdom truth forms the foundation of the curriculum, and such truth must be presented in real-life settings. Remember, as already pointed out, the church today confronts people who have embraced a radically different worldview from that of their parents and grandparents. The church, therefore, must learn to present God's message in a way that speaks to contemporary people. Moreover, good Christian education sets forth the biblical meaning and demands of discipleship. Only as Christ speaks through his committed disciples will the gospel take effect. Godliness cannot be separated from evangelism.

Therefore the third element that must be recognized is that an adequate Christian education program must grow out of the pressing needs of people where they are in today's world. The great temptation in Christian education revolves around becoming too content-centered rather than person-centered. People are what matter to God. And, as we have seen, postmoderns relate to people. So the church finds itself thrust back on the principle of relational evangelism.

Fourth, the function of Christian education should help believers fulfill God's intention for their lives. This idea will be expanded as we discuss the actual nature of accomplishing one's ministry in a life of outreach.

Finally, and as a capsule of the above principles, Christian education must be seen more broadly than just equipping the church for its own existence. It must be expansive enough to reach out into the unbelieving community and confront people with God's revealed truth. The kingdom of God constitutes the vision and goal. Jesus the Teacher serves as an obvious example of this principle. Our Lord reached out to all people, declaring, "the kingdom of heaven is at hand" (Matt. 4:17). Leonard Griffith has well said, "This man outside the church . . . challenges us to reach him and commend our faith to him. He challenges us simply because he is there just as Mount Everest challenged adventurous men until they finally conquered it."[8] And to carry the simile on, if the local church made the preparation and effort in its Christian education program of outreach in as dedicated a fashion as did Sir Edmund Hillary and his party who first conquered Mount Everest, the results would be similar. The church can reach the summit.

A comprehensive Christian education program of that magnitude obviously calls for mature and imaginative leadership. This means many congregations will have to trust God to raise up leaders before the task of educating the bulk of the laity can begin. There is a real place for the effective minister/leader in this body; the team needs a good coach. But that pressing need must not deter a beginning. A start can be made.

What then are the qualities to look for and attempt to create in those who lead? Much has been written on leadership in recent years. A brief outline will suffice here. One pastor, Rev. R. Rodney Collins, has set forth ten qualifications for leadership:

1. A humble dependence on God whose Holy Spirit guides into all the truth (John 16:13). A young married couple leading an international Bible study group in a church confessed, "If we try to do it in our own strength, we get flustered and frustrated. We have learned to trust the Lord to help us."
2. A readiness to stir up (2 Tim. 1:6) and not neglect (1 Tim. 4:14) one's gifts.
3. An appreciation of the place of comprehensive Christian education in the church's life, in accordance with the Great Commission, "Make disciples . . . teaching them" (the present participle implying a continuous process, not only preparing believers for baptism but continuing afterward with a view to practical Christian living).
4. Teachability, especially in regard to modern educational techniques and methods. "Give instruction to a wise man, and he will be still wiser" (Prov. 9:9 RSV). "You then who teach others, will you not teach yourself?" (Rom. 2:21 RSV).
5. Faithfulness, rather than exceptional ability. "Faithful men . . . will be able to teach others also" (2 Tim. 2:2 RSV).
6. A love of people and a real concern for them, rather than passion for talking to them!
7. A respect for others that enables one to accept criticism and profit by it (Rom. 12:3).
8. Sensitivity in personal relationships. The good and efficient work of a dedicated leader can be vitiated if his relations with others lack a sensitive awareness of their feelings, needs, and desires.
9. The ability to deal with personality problems, especially those arising out of the voluntary nature of Christian service.
10. An optimistic spirit inspired by Christian hope, which will not easily be depressed by difficulties, disappointments, and discouragements.[9]

These ten qualifications may seem a large order, and they may never be completely attained; still, worthy goals give direction when taken seriously.

It will be good right here to pause for a moment and summarize what has been called for up to this point. The issue revolves around the biblical principle that the entire body of the church has received the commission to evangelize its age. In this light, the laity must be equipped for the task; hence the stress on the importance and nature of Christian education. But before the mass of church members can be taught, mature leaders must be developed so that they may adequately teach others. And the present leaders have the responsibility to "get the ball rolling." This calls for what is commonly called church administration and programming. But underlying it all rests the leadership, wisdom, and power of the Holy Spirit as he forms Christ within (Gal. 4:19) the serving body of Christ. Thus God's people fix their hands to the plowshare, and the leaders set the pattern to turn the soil of the organizational phase of the task.

Church Administration and Organization in Mission

Administration seems to be an unspiritual concept, at least for some pastors and leaders. The question has been raised, "Is administration not outside the minister's *spiritual* call?" Perhaps it may help to realize what actually constitutes church administration. Alvin Lindgren defines the enterprise in these words:

> Purposeful church administration is the involvement of the church in the discovery of her nature and mission and in moving in a coherent and comprehensive manner toward providing such experience as will enable the church to utilize all her resources and personnel in the fulfillment of her mission of making known God's love for all men.[10]

That is hardly "unspiritual," and surely the Spirit of God will raise up some in the church who can assume such responsibilities. Even a secular definition of administration has significant implications for a church when its principles are translated into the life of a Spirit-directed Christian congregation. For example, Ordway Tead tells us:

> Administration is the process and agency which is responsible for the determination of the aims for which an organization and its management are to strive, which establishes the broad policies under which they are to operate, and which gives general oversight to the continuing effectiveness of the total operation in reaching the objectives sought.[11]

If one understands the nature and purpose of mission, such a task is mandatory for God's servants. W. L. Howse has well stated:

Equipping God's People for the Task   141

For years many leaders have felt that administration was fine for the business world but that it was too secular for churches. The recognition of administration as a church process will remove the stigma of secularism and make administration a useful tool for churches. Good administration is nothing more than following correct processes in getting essential work done well.[12]

Administration thus assumes an important role in ministry in today's world. God's people need to be trained to reach our emerging postmodern world. It cannot be minimized. A myriad of fine authors have recently produced books on church leadership. For example, Rick Warren, John Maxwell, and George Barna have produced excellent books on the subject. Leaders should be zealous to be informed in their task, and church leaders must be committed to equipping the saints for the work of the ministry (Eph. 4:12). But what makes up the structures of ministry that are to be created? To this important issue we now turn.

Gifts of the Spirit and Organization for Ministry

The biblical theme of the church evangelizing and ministering on the basis of the gifts of the Spirit has been written on extensively. Therefore, only an outline of the subject will be presented here. This does not minimize, however, the truth of spiritual gifts and their vital importance in reaching people for Christ. Moreover, not every church has risen to the challenge of this biblical concept. Therefore, a brief reiteration of it is in order.

Perhaps the reason administration and leadership have often seemed rather tedious chores is because of the problem of finding a truly satisfying way to organize the local church into effective ministry. So often it appears that organizing is merely for organization's sake, and little satisfaction can be found in organizing a church simply to keep the machine running. It can even seem at times that church programming has degenerated into manipulating people. That can result in putting square pegs in round holes, and as a result no one is genuinely satisfied and the work suffers. A beautiful pattern of effective Christian ministry emerges in the Bible, however, and is one that can be employed by the dynamic of the Holy Spirit who works to accomplish the mission. If such is the case, full satisfaction and success can be expected. The biblical principle Paul labored to implement in the churches centers in Christians serving their Lord in the context of the gifts of the Spirit—the charismata.

One must be careful here, however. Perversions of the teaching have touched not a few churches. But laying those problems aside, the sin-

gle most important fact to realize is that these gifts of the Spirit are given
to the church *for ministry*. They are by and large not for individual spiritual indulgence. Of course, some are more individually oriented than
others, but the Holy Spirit imparts them essentially so that believers
may prove effective in their service for Christ. If this principle is kept in
mind, the church can save itself from errors.

The concept of using the gifts of the Spirit for ministry held significant prominence in the life and ministry of the early church. Three rather
lengthy passages are devoted to the principle in Paul's writings: Romans
12:3–8; 1 Corinthians 12–14; Ephesians 4:4–16. A number of things need
to be said concerning the concept.

The New Testament declares that when Christ ascended back to the
Father, "He led captive a host of captives, and He gave gifts to men" (Eph.
4:8). These gifts are the consequence of the presence of the "Spirit of promise" who indwells all believers. As previously pointed out, they are given
by our Lord primarily for the purpose of equipping his people for the work
of the ministry. Distinguishing these *gifts* of the Spirit from the *fruit* of
the Spirit (Gal. 5:22–23) is important. The fruit are the manifestation of
the Spirit in the daily life of the Christian, making him or her Christlike
in character. The gifts are the manifestation of the Spirit through the
believer for effective service. In a word, they are "ministering gifts."

Spiritual gifts are enumerated in the three primary New Testament passages mentioned above. First, in Ephesians 4:11 we find the following:

1. apostles
2. prophets
3. evangelists
4. pastors/teachers

Romans 12:6–8 has in addition:

1. prophecy
2. service
3. teaching
4. exhortation
5. giving
6. leading
7. showing mercy

In 1 Corinthians 12:8–10, 28 we find:

1. word of wisdom
2. word of knowledge

3. faith
4. healing
5. miracles
6. prophecy
7. distinguishing of spirits
8. various tongues
9. interpretation of tongues
10. helps
11. administrations

From the above lists, it becomes evident that the principle of the gifts of the Spirit has profound significance for the *entire* work of the ministry. Paul says, "It is important, brethren, that you should have clear knowledge on the subject of spiritual gifts" (1 Cor. 12:1 WEYMOUTH). What can be said about these gifts?

The Nature of the Gifts

First of all, some gifts are obviously Christians themselves with particular ministries, for example, apostles, prophets, and teachers. In other cases, the emphasis rests on the gift itself rather than on the individual who has received the gift, for example, faith and various tongues. Yet this distinction should not be pressed too far. Perhaps the simplest thing to say is that a gift apart from a believer to exercise the gift makes for an abstraction, and a believer must have a gift to be an effective Christian servant. The gift and the gifted form the warp and woof of the theme.

Further, the gifts of the Spirit are not to be confused with natural talents. Although people have natural abilities—abilities that God will surely use in his service—spiritual gifts are not these per se. Marcus Dods points this up by stating, "They [the believers] were endowed at their conversion . . . with certain powers which they had not previously possessed, and which were due to the influence of the Holy Spirit."[13]

The gifts must further be seen as spiritual powers that the believer exercises only under the control of the Holy Spirit. They are not to be used simply when and how the believer may wish, let alone to enjoy selfishly. Alfred Plummer declares, "The Operator . . . is always God: every one of the gifts in every person that manifests them . . . is bestowed and set in motion by Him."[14] Paul wrote the lengthy passage found in 1 Corinthians 12–14 to direct the use of the gifts and to save the church from abuses.

To summarize, the gifts must be understood as grace-gifts, supernatural endowments, spiritual manifestations of God the Spirit through the believer for the enrichment of the body and the development and work of the ministry. As has been said, "It is simply the Holy Spirit working through us in a given manner, at the time He, the Spirit, chooses, for the carrying out of the ministry to which we have been appointed of God."[15] E. P. Gould states, "They are all, however various, to be employed in the service of Him, the one Lord."[16] Moreover, it must be strongly emphasized that the Holy Spirit distributes gifts *to every believer*. Paul states there are no exceptions; every believer has a gift or gifts. R. C. H. Lenski declares that the emphasis rests primarily on the dative in 1 Corinthians 12:7, implying that "to each one . . . each believer has his gifts, and every bestowal of a gift is for the common good."[17]

The Purpose of Each Gift

At this point in our discussion, we need to understand the actual meaning of each gift and the purpose for which God intends it. The following list, from *The New Testament Order for Church and Missionary* by Alexander Rattray Hay, offers a general classification:

1. For the proclamation of God's self-disclosure: the gift of prophecy or preaching.
2. For teaching the divine revelation: the gift of teaching.
3. For enabling God's blessing to flow into needy lives: the gift of faith that enables believers to rest upon God's promises and trust in the power that is beyond the sphere of human possibilities.
4. For the revelation of God's will and purpose in matters: the gift of wisdom so that God's purpose in His word can be grasped.
5. For understanding the practical application of eternal principles in daily experience: the utterance of knowledge.
6. For protection against evil: the gift of discernment of spirits.
7. For the practical manifestation of the love of Christ there are three gifts: mercy, the Paraclete gift [the gift of the Holy Spirit's comfort], and giving.
8. For maintaining order in the life and work of the church: the gift of government. [This is surely not far from what we spoke about when we discussed the importance of church leadership and administration.]
9. For help in the community: the gift of serviceable ministries or "helps."
10. As special signs of God's power and presence, there are four gifts: miracles, healing, tongues, and interpretation of tongues.[18]

A few things should be said concerning this brief outline and the purpose of the gifts. The number of gifts found in the Scriptures is comparatively small. This leads to the conclusion that each gift listed must be understood as a designation of a class of gifts. In each classification there will be many variations. Circumstances, situations, and needs differ from culture to culture and from generation to generation. There are probably hundreds of individual, specific gifts. The biblical gifts must be seen as flexible in their manifestations so as to meet the relevant needs of all people at all times. This clearly speaks to our postmodern culture. Also, a study of all the gifts of the Spirit makes it evident that God has provided in full measure for all needs of the church in its growth, worship, evangelism, and ministry. The organization of the local church, its government, its instruction and equipping, its worship, its ministry of witness, and its entire corporate life of ministry are fully cared for. As John Short has said: "Let there be among the Corinthian Christians, and in every Christian church in any age, clear recognition of the simple truth that in such a divinely appointed organism as the body of Christ, for its vitality and its effective witness, a variety of functions is required."[19] And if the church is open to his lead, the Spirit of God will surely see to it that no part of the work suffers for lack of a gift.

Furthermore, the principle of spiritual gifts is what makes the local church a balanced, well-proportioned body of Christ. G. G. Findlay points out that the charismata of the Spirit are "portioned out amongst the members of Christ, for manifold and reciprocal service to His body."[20] Paul set the entire theme in this important context when he states that the Holy Spirit bestows these gifts "as he wills" (1 Cor. 12:11 RSV). Surely he will not create a body that is all hands or eyes or feet or tongues. That would be a monstrosity, not a body at all. He will develop a perfectly functioning and unified body. Actually, a church never becomes a unified whole by mere organization alone; the Spirit fashions believers into a body. William Barclay states in commenting on the Corinthian church, "The whole idea of Paul . . . is to stress the essential unity of the church."[21]

Finally, when *the whole church* employs their gifts under the direction of the Holy Spirit, the church is built up in the faith and strengthened in the work, and the *missio Dei*, the mission of God, is carried on. As the entire church exercises their gifts, the whole witnessing body makes a unified impact for Christ. As Lenski has said, "Each member of the church benefits the entire body by rightly employing his *particular* gift."[22] The work is God's mission, and the New Testament makes it very clear that the work is energized by the Spirit through the whole *gifted* church. Therein the stress lies.

It is my hope that this short discussion has made obvious what a church is like when it functions on the basis of the gifts of the Spirit. As

Barclay says, "The picture we get is the picture of a Church vividly alive. Things happened; in fact astonishing things happened. Life was heightened and intensified and sensitized. There was nothing flat and dull and ordinary about the . . . Church."[23] This constitutes what we all desire today for the body and what we must practice if we are to evangelize our contemporary postmodern generation effectively.

The Pragmatics of the Theme

In the light of all that has been said concerning spiritual gifts, the principle emerges that the church should be geared in its organizational life so that all the members of the church can exercise the gifts that have been committed to them by the Holy Spirit. It may be that this is already being done to some degree implicitly, but an *explicit* structuring of the organizational pattern of the local church along these lines is needed. In other words, the church's program should be developed in such a manner that the Holy Spirit can manifest himself in and through his people as he wills. We need "gift structures," not just programs. This obviously calls for a number of revolutionary approaches.

Initially the church must place confidence in its gifted members. As one layman has expressed it:

> Why is it the Church today will not trust its members? Why does the Church so often decline to recognize and to accept the activity of the Spirit among unregulated groups of Christians? Why is all initiative in the Church expected and presumed to derive from the clergy? It is because we have substituted for the biblical doctrine of the Holy Spirit as ruler in the Church, a doctrine of our own, unknown to scripture, the authority of professionalism. In regard to the conducting of services and the administration of the sacraments the authority of the ministry is not in question. But we are now considering the training and commissioning of Christian men and women to take lay initiative in the world.[24]

If we take seriously the lay-centered ministry concept, and genuinely believe that God's Spirit empowers and gives gifts to all Christians, the church must trust these believers to get on with the job. After all, this is what the Bible means by the priesthood of all believers. Priesthood in the scriptural sense means ministry as well as personal access to God's presence. Moreover, such an approach saves laypeople from feeling inadequate for the task. When a person discovers he or she has a gift, that Christian becomes motivated as never before.

As implied, this means there will probably be significant change in the present structures of most local churches. A real revolution will occur in many congregations; it will mean beginning with people instead of programs. Gifted people come first; then programming to exercise their gifts follows. It will mean refusing to prop up old, irrelevant, inept structures and meeting real needs of real people. Postmoderns will respond to that. In the concluding section of this chapter, some guidelines will be considered.

To implement the principle, leaders must give considerable instruction, biblical teaching, and help. Most Christians seem relatively uninstructed concerning the work of the Holy Spirit. Many of God's people do not even know they are gifted by the Holy Spirit, let alone understand what gifts the Spirit would manifest through them. An in-depth process of education on pneumatology is needed. It may well be that many misconceptions concerning the work of the Holy Spirit will have to be eradicated. The church must be on guard to protect people from being swept away in some movement that says it is of the Holy Spirit but bears little fruit of the Spirit. Not a few Christians have fallen victim to errors here. As Paul stood on guard for the believers in Corinth, so also must the contemporary church, if we would reach the new generation.

This can all be summarized by stating that the *missio Dei* is committed to the whole body; and the entire church, recognizing that every member is gifted by the Spirit, engages in the ministry of the Word. To state it again, the structures of the church must be set up so that each member can serve in relation to his or her specific gift. And all believers need development of their gifts through Christian education. When it all comes together, the church emerges as a truly unified, functioning body being built up in the faith. In this context, the work of ministry-evangelism goes forward. But can it be accomplished in today's traditional congregations, or even in the so-called "seeker sensitive" churches with their more free-flowing worship styles?

Some Practical Suggestions

If God has called all his people into ministry, then surely the bulk of God's people can be led and equipped to perform their God-given task. Therefore, some practical suggestions on how to develop a church-centered evangelistic program are in order. Such a program will call for honesty and bravery, but it must be undertaken. As one pastor said, "The world will not be won by people who stand around wringing their hands." The call sounds forth for action. The suggestions that follow may be a mere beginning, but they have been undertaken by others, and God has honored the honest effort.

From the standpoint of the corporate service of the church, many of the present structures of church life may need changing. How can this hurdle be cleared? There is always resistance—often strong resistance—to change. It can begin by spiritual church leaders coming together in an attitude of openness. It would be best in most instances to create a representative group from the structured life of the church—the directors of the various departmental aspects of the church program. But above all, let them be the ones who are spiritually minded and open to the purposes of God in reaching for Christ the contemporary, postmodern world—the future of the church.

Then, after the leaders have been reasonably taught and oriented, they can begin teaching, encouraging, challenging, and informing the rest of the church (2 Tim. 2:2). It must be pressed home that the need of evangelism and openness is required if the church is going to be effectively geared for outreach. The leadership group should be made vividly aware of the goals and the mission purpose of the church. Then they can pass it on to the rest of the congregation. A church needs to know where to go. Of course, if the church has never written a statement of purpose, it must begin there.

Then after much prayer, education, and heart-searching, leaders who are genuinely committed to mission and zealous for it should sit down together with their purpose before them and scrutinize the entire present church program. Let them examine and evaluate each and every facet of the structured life of the church. Let them be honest about each phase, asking these questions: Does it line up with the mission statement and goals of the church? Does it really have relevance for today's world? Does it honestly meet needs? Does it genuinely further the kingdom of God through the life of the church? Does it accord with scriptural principles, such as the exercising of spiritual gifts? These are not easy questions to ask. They call for objectivity, integrity, and not a little courage. We all have vested interests in our present church structures, and to be objective and honest is often painful. But it is essential that the leadership analyze what the church is doing in the light of what, under God, it *should* be doing. In the appendix section of this book a guide for conducting such a survey is given (see appendix B). Many churches have followed such an approach and found it most helpful.

Two vital principles must be paramount in this endeavor: (1) The church's mission and purpose goals must be clearly grasped by the group—and the church as a whole. (2) The new structures must be built on the principle of involving all church members and allowing them to exercise their gifts. This implies that attention will be given to "go-structures" (going to the world) more than "come-structures" (merely inviting them to come to us), at least as far as evangelistic outreach is concerned.

It cannot be emphasized too strongly that the educational process integrating all the aforementioned principles in the whole church must be patiently followed. It is essential that God's people be educated in the principles and involved in the divine task. It will take time and courageous sacrifice. But remember, God's kingdom progress hangs to some degree in the balance.

One final word of caution: The tentative program to be implemented must be kept flexible. Some new programs may prove unsuccessful when they are actually implemented. If such is the case, let the church be brave once again and eliminate them. The mistake of getting wedded to the new program can be as deadly as being wedded to the old. The local church must be subject to constant change in its programming if it is to improve its methodologies and keep abreast of the ever-changing community.

Some Practical Examples

Small Groups

A few examples of success in innovative outreach may prove helpful and inspirational. One of the most productive methods of outreach for the younger set is the small group. Of course, this approach is not new as a principle. It can be traced right back to the New Testament house church. John Wesley used it, having adapted it from the pietists of Germany. Lately, however, there has been new interest in small groups. For many churches they have become very fruitful endeavors, appealing to the younger postmoderns. Small groups put the ministry on a more personal, relational level. They have been particularly successful in difficult inner-city areas. Often there are key laypeople in the church who can develop a regular program of small meetings. These leaders keep their homes open at all times and have regularly structured group meetings. Of course, the gifted leader must learn to be flexible and not be shocked or put off by what he or she hears from those who attend. Postmoderns are different. But if the leaders can communicate to their attendees that they truly care and understand them, results can be most rewarding.

Again, let it be said that most conventional methodologies will not reach the multitude of young postmoderns today. The church must learn to accept the new generation as they are and let them express themselves in their own way. If their music, dress, and language are strange to the older generation, it does not necessarily mean they are wrong. And young postmoderns are open to the gospel in a way some older generations were not. They are asking serious questions. They are interested in at least some form of "spirituality." May the church be compassionate, imaginative, and zealous in reaching them. If it requires unusual things, may God's people be mature enough to employ methods that communicate to the new culture. Using small groups as just one such method, imaginative churches and their leaders will have much success reaching the new generation by many methods.

Person-to-Person Ministry

Every community has its own peculiar needs. Delinquency, crime, drugs, illegitimacy, minority groups, underprivileged areas, ethnic groups, the isolated wealthy, needy subcultural groups, all these and many other needs can be discovered. The local church should attempt to step into these gaps and minister. For a concrete illustration, see appendix A.

People of all ages respond to manifestations of genuine Christian love and acceptance. The person-to-person ministry must be utilized, and members can be educated to perform it. Personal witnessing, for example, emerges as vital and expected of all. In this area church members need to be challenged and trained to share their faith. Witnessing in the context of meeting pressing needs often opens the door for a reception of the gospel. To repeat John Stott, "A hungry man has no ears." Personal witnessing is often the most effective way to confront the postmoderns with the gospel. This calls for building relationships, which can often be done by the meeting of needs.

Relatively few postmoderns are now attending church. The factory worker speaking about Christ to his coworkers, the young person giving the Good News to his or her friends—these are the ones who will make the greatest impact on contemporary society. It will take time, effort, and sacrifice. Relationships are costly. If only God could open our mouths. On this theme, Wilson Carlile said, "I have got the biggest job I have ever tackled in my life. I am trying to open the mouths of people in the pews."[25] It hardly seems an overstatement to say that either the mouths of God's people will be opened and relationships established, or the church may well slip into even more serious decline. There are ample effective training programs today to inspire and equip those who would witness for Christ.

An illustration of what one person can accomplish as a personal witness is the story of M. L. O'Neal. This man grew into a most effective witness for Christ. He was a layman with limited education; he had to drop out of school at twelve years of age to go to work in the fields of the family farm. He was not a great Bible scholar, though he faithfully read his Bible. He was anything but a skilled theologian. His most remarkable quality lay in his ability to help others to faith in Christ. This quality developed out of his ardent passion to win the unconverted. He seized every opportunity to share Christ. He would bear his testimony in every conceivable context. He would witness to waitresses in restaurants, clerks in stores—wherever he met people. So skillful was he that he rarely offended anyone, and he led literally hundreds to faith in the Lord Jesus Christ. His whole life revolved around this one passion. A misunderstanding psychiatrist would probably say he was a compulsive or obsessive personality. But here was one layman, totally committed to sharing the gospel, and God used him significantly. The key is getting involved in the lives of people, loving them, and pointing them to Christ. Relational evangelism is a vital approach in today's new culture.

Service

When Christians are encouraged and equipped to demonstrate Christ's love in deeds of kindness, countless opportunities will arise. God's people are gifted by the Spirit to serve. Wherever there is a need, some Christian can step in. As an example of this type of service, in one of my pastorates there was a dear lady, very poor by most standards, with a rather unstable husband, but she excelled in doing little helpful things for people. She was never able to do big things—finances prohibited that. Yet she was always doing what she could and was loved and appreciated for it. Her spirit of genuine Christlikeness in meeting needs was inspirational. She had the gift of helps. In the exercising of one's gift, great evangelism can ensue. Surely Christians can be led to emulate this principle in their daily lives. All are gifted. In the context of service, doors are open for evangelism as never before.

The list of evangelistic outreach methods could go on, but may the entire congregation discover what God is leading the church to do, corporately and individually, and thus intelligently cooperate with the Holy Spirit. God is in this world ministering; the church should be there with him. Let us break out of the four walls of our buildings and meet this new postmodern world. The church has been gifted by the Holy Spirit to do just that. May the church leaders rise to their role to aid God's people in discovering their gifts and thus fulfilling their respective role (see appendix C for help here). That is the responsibility of the leadership

(Eph. 4:11–12). Construct programs that present opportunities for people to discover their gifts, and then encourage and help the gifted laity develop their gifts and use them wisely as servants and witnesses for Christ. It is a large task but one vital to kingdom extension. On this basis the Holy Spirit will surely lead the church and its individual members into avenues of effective service and evangelistic outreach that will prove powerful for God's glory and the winning of people to faith in our Lord. Can we rise to the challenge? The final chapter will present the answer.

Questions and Issues for Study

1. Who is to be engaged in the task of evangelizing postmoderns and why?
2. How does one get equipped for the task?
3. What place does the Bible play in all this?
4. What place does prayer play in all this?
5. What place does a godly life play in all this?
6. What place does the Holy Spirit play in all this?
7. How do you discover your gift of ministry?
8. How do you develop your gift?
9. How does the church figure in all this? How does it all relate to evangelism?
10. What do you intend to do in light of these biblical realities?

nine

Spiritual Power for the Work

We have seen how the spiritually healthy church, a congregation that has the ring of Christ's reality and presence, communicates to postmoderns. With the postmodern negative feelings concerning institutionalism—including the institutionalized church—if our congregations do not radiate Jesus Christ, few are going to be reached for our Lord. Therefore, this final chapter serves as something of an appeal for evangelizing the postmodern world with the power of a true Christian spirituality. After all, that is the bottom line for all Christian service.

Although some space has already been given to this theme, it cannot be emphasized too strongly that the people of God who would evangelize all generations effectively must never forget that the Lord's work goes forward, "Not by might nor by power, but by My Spirit" (Zech. 4:6). That is ultimately how postmoderns and others can and will be reached, and ample power exists to be successful in the mission. Resources are available on which the leaders or any Christian can call that will enable

153

him or her to make a significant impact for Christ and the gospel. And simply put, that is what the *missio Dei* is all about.

The Power of a Holy Life

When one's Christian service—and the service of the church as a whole—is finally summed up, that which makes the most lasting and vital impression on the world centers in a Christ-like life and vibrant testimony. This principle holds for the individual believer and the church collectively. As a young minister, I once had the opportunity of serving as associate pastor to a true man of God. This man was not the pastor of a large, influential church, nor was he an outstanding or eloquent preacher. His intellectual achievements were not extraordinary. Yet his ministry impacted a large area. Many came to faith in Christ through his and the church's faithful witness. The fact that his ministry, and that of the church he so inspired, proved outstanding was because of the profound godliness of his congregation's life. Although he passed on some years ago, the man's testimony and that of the church remain. These realities imply several things.

In the first place, the *image* of the church in any community or culture relates directly to the effectiveness of its ministry. As one writer has said, "Image communication can have an important supporting role to play."[1] This stands true for the church generally, leaders and laypeople alike. Recognizing this important principle, Paul said, "Brethren, join in imitating me, and mark those who so live as you have an example in us" (Phil. 3:17 RSV). When any believer can honestly make such a statement, his or her life and service will prove powerful in mission. The church must image Jesus Christ.

Further, native ability is not necessarily the determining factor in effective evangelistic service. God obviously uses his gifted people, but as long as one's life is totally committed to Christ's lordship, God will make that life useful in leading others. Therefore, all who aspire to be instrumental in evangelism must learn the principles of godly living. The principles are few but elemental. The entire concept can be summarized as simply knowing God in the experiential fellowship of Jesus Christ. As John in his first epistle put it:

> What was from the beginning, what we have heard, what we have seen with our eyes, what we have looked at and touched with our hands, concerning the Word of Life—and the life was manifested, and we have seen and testify and proclaim to you the eternal life, which was with the Father and was manifested to us—what we have seen and heard we proclaim to you also, so that you too may have fellowship with us; and indeed our fel-

lowship is with the Father, and with His Son Jesus Christ. These things
we write, so that our joy may be made complete.

This is the message we have heard from Him and announce to you, that
God is Light, and in Him there is no darkness at all. . . . if we walk in the
Light as He Himself is in the Light, we have fellowship with one another,
and the blood of Jesus His Son cleanses us from all sin.

1 John 1:1–5, 7

From this passage it becomes clear that daily fellowship with Christ
constitutes the essence of knowing God. The "abiding" principle is foundational for the individual believer as well as for the church as a body.
This basic idea can be illustrated in the experience of a young minister
who, as the story goes, much admired the ministry of an aged man of God
who was to bring an address in his city. The young minister, thinking that
perhaps he could discover some secret that would unravel the mystery of
the tremendous success of the old minister, went to the service, seeking
that which would give him insight to a similarly effective life of service.
When the time of the service arrived, however, the aged preacher, though
present, was not well and could not deliver his message. Nonetheless, the
convener of the meeting prevailed on the elderly gentleman to say just a
word. As the old servant came to the podium, it seemed as though the
presence of Christ settled down on the entire congregation. He then made
one simple statement: "I'm glad that I know God." These words fell like a
hammer on the heart of the young minister. *That's it,* he exclaimed to himself. *That's his secret. This man truly knows God.*

Most would agree that the young minister made a correct analysis of
the situation. If our lives and that of the church are to prove effective
and successful as God counts success, if we are to make a spiritual impact
on our communities and our world, modern or postmodern, we must
come into a living knowledge and true fellowship with God himself. In
a word, we must come to know God vitally and dynamically.

Several things need to be said concerning the possibility of knowing
God in the sense of living daily in his presence. Initially, it must be understood that as John saw it, Christianity is neither a speculative system of
thought nor simply a mystical existential experience. It centers in a mys-
ticism of genuine communion with God as revealed objectively in his
Son Jesus Christ and the principles thereof recorded in the Word of God.
"Grace and truth" (John 1:14) come together in the experience of abiding in Christ.

John views such fellowship with God as a marvel, marvelous because
of the fact that "God is Light, and in Him there is no darkness at all"
(1 John 1:5). The metaphor concerning the character of God as light can
be found in various places in the New Testament. The figure of light

obviously refers to God's holiness, power, and grace—the essence of his being. His "otherness," as some theologians express it, gets to the point. From various New Testament passages, where this figure is drawn, something of the marvel of what it means to walk with God in the light can be grasped.

First, God is complete light. John put it this way: "In Him there is no darkness at all." God is completely and unequivocally morally perfect. His righteousness is infinite and ultimate. He is absolute holiness. In him is no darkness at all.

Not only is the light that surrounds the Godhead infinite and ultimate, it is also unchangeable light, for God himself is immutable. James wrote, "Every good thing given and every perfect gift is from above, coming down from the Father of lights, with whom there is no variation or shifting shadow" (James 1:17). God never changes. How different we are. The moral and spiritual tone of our lives can go from the heights to the depths. But God's holy light is utterly unchanging. He can always be experienced as "the same yesterday and today and forever" (Heb. 13:8). He is always consistent light.

Paul further states that the light surrounding God is unapproachable. The apostle wrote in 1 Timothy 6:15–16: "The King of kings and Lord of lords . . . alone possesses immortality and dwells in unapproachable light, whom no man has seen or can see." A new appreciation of the holiness, sovereignty, and majesty of the God of light is a needed contemporary realization. The current rather humanistic overtones about God we often hear, even in our churches and some of their music, bring the God of holy glory down to a level certainly not found in the Scriptures. A fresh vision of the glory and holiness of God like that which Isaiah experienced stands as a real need today. When the prophet saw God for all he actually is, he fell on his face in the dust crying out, "Woe is me, for I am ruined!" (Isa. 6:5). God is light and his holiness is utterly unapproachable by sinful mankind in the flesh. Though he is intimate and concerned for us all, he resides in absolute holiness. That makes the possibility of fellowship with God a glorious wonder. God is light, and we are darkness, the very antithesis of light. We hardly need to be reminded that we are often found walking in sin's darkness. Nevertheless, we can actually walk in the light of God's wondrous presence. That is a marvel. How can it be?

Fellowship through Confession

Fellowship with God can be seen in the Bible as a glorious possibility. Yet it must obviously be worked out in the dynamic of everyday experience. Foundational to the pragmatic implementation of the experience of "walking in the light" rests the realization that fellowship with God begins with confession of all known sins. John tells us:

> If we say we have fellowship with Him and yet walk in darkness, we lie and do not practice the truth; but if we walk in the Light as He Himself is in the Light, we have fellowship with one another, and the blood of Jesus His Son cleanses us from all sin. If we say that we have no sin, we are deceiving ourselves and the truth is not in us. If we confess our sins, He is faithful and righteous to forgive us our sins and to cleanse us from all unrighteousness.
>
> 1 John 1:6–9

From the historical perspective, John was dealing with the error of the Gnostic idea that human flesh was sinful in and of itself. In fact these thinkers held that anything material was tainted with sin. This brought them into heretical concepts relative to the person of Christ and to grave moral errors concerning their own conduct.

The Gnostics could not conceive that the Son of God actually came in the flesh. They denied the incarnation. They felt that as long as the flesh was sinful, God could be interested only in the spirit. Thus moral laxity was permissible. Thankfully, Gnosticism as a philosophical system has largely passed away, but the sin issue surely has not. Even for Christians, sin intrudes as an ever present dilemma. And if God's people do not learn how to deal with sin as it invades their experience, vital fellowship with God is just as unreal a dream for believers as it was for the Gnostics. God is light and cannot sanction sin.

How, then, does one deal with this problem of sin? The essential answer to our quandary can be found in verse 7: "If we walk in the Light as He Himself is in the Light, we have fellowship with one another, and the blood of Jesus His Son cleanses us from all sin." The key phrase in the verse is the final statement where John says the blood of Jesus, God's Son, *continually* (present tense) cleanses from all sin. This simply means that if God's people aspire to walk in the light, there must be constant cleansing by the power of Christ's forgiveness. Could it be that the proclamation of the death of Christ as the remedy for the sinful life has been restricted to the historical past alone, to the time when Christ was first trusted as Lord and Savior? As wonderful and vital as the conversion experience is, John declares that Christians are to be constantly, daily cleansed by the blood of Christ. The death of Christ was efficacious not only on the day of conversion when our *relationship* with God was established (John 1:12), but his sacrifice stands effectual in forgiveness every day to maintain *fellowship* with him (1 John 1:3). Sanctification, as well as justification, comes through the blood of Christ and the power of the Holy Spirit. Christians must learn the importance of this work of God in their experience and recognize the centrality of the daily cleansing from sins by Jesus' blood. In this alone, walking with God can be realized. Our cleansing dispels darkness so we can walk in the light.

We probably all agree to these basic truths, yet right here nebulous thinking can easily creep in. It seems too few have actually grasped the biblical concept of how the believer is to deal with his or her sins so that the blood of Christ may be efficacious in cleansing and thus keeping the believer in fellowship with God. This idea calls for an investigation in a little more depth.

Dealing with Sin

Experiencing the cleansing of one's sins centers in a proper understanding and evaluation of how sin manifests itself in life's basic relationships. It must be recognized that sin usually intrudes itself in a threefold relational manner. All sin involves the Christian and his or her relationship to God. And some sin involves not only the Christian and God but also his or her relationship to another individual. There can also be sin that involves the Christian and a group of people, such as the church. Even though at times other individuals may be involved, every sin is basically and essentially an affront to God.

When Christians see their daily sin as nebulous and indefinite, they are normally not moved to deal with it in God's prescribed manner. We must recognize our sins are specific and individual acts of rebellion and then identify any person or persons we have offended. When sin is seen in this way, it can be dealt with accordingly and scripturally, for the Bible teaches how to deal with sin on such a basis. For example, concerning the problem of sin as it involves the believer alone and his or her personal fellowship with God, John tells us, "If we confess our sins, He is faithful and righteous to forgive us our sins and to cleanse us from all unrighteousness" (1 John 1:9).

All sin must be confessed to God. The word *confess* is a compound term composed of the verb "to say" and the prefix "the same." This implies that to confess sins is "to say the same as" or "to assent to" the convicting Spirit of God that the *particular, specific* thing of which the Spirit of God is convicting us actually is a sin. To confess sins scripturally is "to concede to" or "to agree with" the voice of God that a specific behavior—for the Spirit of God deals with specifics in the Christian's life—truly is a sin. This precludes a "blanket" confession of sins. For example, we may often pray, "Lord, forgive me of all my sins." Such a prayer may be acceptable for public worship, but this does not constitute the way the Scriptures state a Christian is to confess privately. We do not commit our sins as a nebulous whole; each is an individual act that offends God. Therefore, we confess them one by one to him.

This clearly implies that we should stay before God, walk in his presence, and permit the Holy Spirit to search us out, convict, and place his finger on those particular deeds that constitute sin. The psalmist prayed, "Search me O God, and know my heart" (Ps. 139:23). Having acknowledged our sins before God in this prescribed manner, we then have the assurance that the blood of Jesus cleanses them all. Of course, we also seek God's forgiveness for the "secret sins" in our lives that we may not be conscious of in the present state of our spiritual perception.

Times of confession should not be understood as morbid, neurotic introspection. This must never be permitted. Biblical confession centers in a simple and honest evaluation of ourselves before God. This brings release and peace.

Some of our sins, of course, offend others as well as God. In these instances, confessing to God alone is insufficient to experience the full release of Christ's forgiveness. We should confess them to God, but Jesus further stated in the Sermon on the Mount (Matthew 5–7) that if you are "presenting your offering at the altar, and there remember that your brother has something against you, leave your offering there before the altar and go; first be reconciled to your brother, and then come and present your offering" (Matt. 5:23–24). One cannot avoid the simple truth presented here. If we sin against another person and our fellowship is thus marred, restitution must be made to that person as well as to God. Jesus' statement surely implies that when we fail to acknowledge sins against individuals to those individuals (as much as possible under present circumstances and as God leads), we cannot expect deep fellowship with God or one another. Moreover, if someone sins against us, we are also to seek restoration with him or her (see Matt. 18:15–17). How blessed the church would be if such honesty and fellowship were maintained. Fellowship is to be sought not only with God, but with one another. That is why John uses the plural in admonition for fellowship (1 John 1:3).

Again, let it be clear, this is no neurotic introspection, seeking and digging out past sins in one's life. And it does not mean, "airing our dirty linen" before the whole world. We must use some discretion and wisdom. Still, we must come to grips with ourselves if we are to have the fullness of fellowship with God and others. Seeking forgiveness from those against whom we have sinned is fundamental in our walking in fellowship with one another. Not only does it get our life right with God, it also keeps us in Christian fellowship with one another. And, after all, that is the ethical thing to do. If we could embrace one another in the arms of confession in the context of a true binding of our lives in love and forgiveness, our homes, our churches, and our nation could be radically changed for the better.

At times we may sin against a group. We may have a particular problem, secret or otherwise, that others could help us with, or it may even be open sin of which a whole group is knowledgeable. In any case, our sin brings reproach on the cause of Christ. How are these issues to be dealt with? James tells us, "Confess your sin to one another, and pray for one another so that you may be healed" (James 5:16). James implies that at times we should confess certain sins to someone, or even to a group in the church or perhaps to the entire congregation as well as to God. This clearly seems to be James's meaning.

There should be some person or group in the fellowship of believers to whom we can be quite open, honest, and candid about ourselves. Is not this the koinonia of love the New Testament talks about? The church should be such a fellowship of love and understanding that we feel unthreatened in opening our real selves to our brothers and sisters in Christ. But let us be most careful here. Again, this must not degenerate into an open airing of our sinful self to the whole world. Some have fallen into this trap. At the same time, however, there is a need of genuine openness among God's people. The principle centers in the fact that sin should be confessed and put right in the context of the offense. We ought to drop the mask we tend to hide behind. As sensitivity to the Holy Spirit is developed and the fellowship of believers deepens, he will surely open the door so that it will become clear what should be shared and with whom. One would hope all our churches could grow into such a fellowship of love, understanding, and healing. Real revival creates that spirit.

If one's sins are so gross and open that reproach is brought on the entire church and the fellowship of the church is thus broken, forgiveness should be sought from the entire church. This is what lies behind the principle of church discipline that many congregations have apparently forgotten today. And this constitutes what a public rededication of one's Christian life should really involve.

Now all of this must be seen in a most positive light. For when it is sanely, maturely, and scripturally approached, confession can become a liberating experience for the individual Christian and the entire church of Christ. Forgiveness and new freedom of soul floods our hearts. When we find ourselves open with God and others, we can be our real selves. There has never been a deep spiritual awakening where this spiritual exercise has not taken place. This gets to the heart of fellowship with Christ and the essence of Christian community.

Victory over Temptation

It is my hope that this discussion concerning sin and confession will not leave the impression that in Christ there is no victory over daily temptations and that our experience of God is nothing more than a continuing cycle of temptation, sin, confession, and forgiveness. The Scriptures are quite clear that God gives power over temptation as we walk in fellowship with him. Paul wrote:

Thanks be to God, who always leads us in triumph in Christ (2 Cor. 2:14).

The law of the Spirit of life in Christ Jesus has set you free from the law of sin and death (Rom. 8:2).

In all these things we overwhelmingly conquer through Him who loved us (Rom. 8:37).

The conclusion can be legitimately drawn from these verses that in Christ victory over daily sin is clearly possible. But how can that victory be achieved? We have surely learned that in our own strength we are powerless against some, if not many, temptations. What is the answer? The church needs to learn the secret because practical holiness of life depends on this truth and an effective evangelistic witness is predicated on it.

The Way of Victory

John deals with the issue of overcoming temptation in his first epistle. He tells us, "This is the victory that has overcome the world—our faith" (1 John 5:4). John says the way to victory travels on the avenue of faith. It does not emerge from our own self-effort or self-determination (Rom. 7:18). Victory comes only through faith. Paul presents the same idea when he states, "Above all [take] the shield of faith, with which you can quench all the flaming darts of the evil one" (Eph. 6:16 RSV) Faith is the victory!

But faith must have an object. It will not do simply to say, "Hav faith!" Genuine faith always has its foundation in truth, God's truth. ᑦ in the matter of victory over sin, in what reality do we place our faiｆ Paul answers that query in Romans 6:1–14 (RSV):

What shall we say then? Are we to continue in sin that grace may abounʿ By no means! How can we who died to sin still live in it? Do you not knᶜ that all of us who have been baptized into Christ Jesus were baptized iʅ his death? We were buried therefore with him by baptism into death, so that as Christ was raised from the dead by the glory of the Father, we too might walk in newness of life. . . .

We know that our old self was crucified with him so that the sinful body might be destroyed, and we might no longer be enslaved to sin. For he who has died is freed from sin. But if we have died with Christ, we believe that we shall also live with him. For we know that Christ being raised from the dead will never die again; death no longer has dominion over him. The death he died he died to sin, once for all, but the life he lives he lives to God. So you also must consider yourselves dead to sin and alive to God in Christ Jesus.

Let not sin therefore reign in your mortal bodies, to make you obey their passions. Do not yield your members to sin as instruments of wickedness, but yield yourselves to God as men who have been brought from death to life, and your members to God as instruments of righteousness. For sin will have no dominion over you, since you are not under law but under grace.

Paul tells us that if a person is dead, that person is freed from sin. When believers die, sin no longer reigns. But at the same time, if we are dead, we will be of no value to Christ's service here on earth. If we could only be dead and alive at the same time, that would solve the dilemma. And right there Paul makes a startling statement. He declares that because of our union with Christ, whereby we have been made one with him, we have shared in our Lord's death on the cross. We are to understand that we have actually died with Christ to sin. In a spiritual sense— yet in a very real way—when Christ died on the cross, we died with him. When he gained the victory by his blood, we shared in that victory by death. The rationale behind this rests in the fact that God sees us as in Christ. New Testament scholar James Stewart demonstrates in his book *A Man in Christ* that to fail to understand what Paul means by "in Christ" means to fail to grasp what Paul means by salvation.[2] The concept of "in Christ" is the key to Pauline theology. In a word, what Christ has experienced, we have experienced. We are *in* him. He died, so we are dead. And as a result, we are free from sin's dominion. Our "old man" has been crucified with Christ (Gal. 2:20).

Furthermore, not only have we died with Christ and shared in that experience of death, because we are "in him," we have also been spiritually resurrected with him. We live a new life because he lives. We are now animated by the resurrected life of our Lord in the person of his Holy Spirit. Can sin thus lord it over the believer? Absolutely not! We are dead to it and alive to God in Christ.

We recognize that this truth does not appeal to pure rationalism. Yet God says it is true, and by *faith* we accept it. In actuality, only faith can grasp this tremendous reality. But therein lies the victory. As one author has pointedly expressed it:

> When Christ died on the cross to sin, we were identified with Him in that death to sin. That is, we died with Him. By our union with Him in His death, we were freed from the penalty of sin and emancipated from the power of sin. All our sanctification therefore must be traced to, and rests upon, the atoning sacrifice of our Lord Jesus Christ. The cross of Christ is the efficient cause of deliverance from the power of sin. Freedom from the dominion of sin is a blessing we may claim by faith, just as we accept pardon.[3]

The Pragmatics

This principle of identification with Christ truly works in everyday experience. For example, let us say we are met by one of our old weaknesses. We have striven to overcome it but with little success. Now, however, we realize our identification with Christ in his death and resurrection and by faith in that fact we say, *This sin has no more power over me. I am dead to it.* Then in faith we look to God alone for the victory, and the resurrected life of Christ (the Holy Spirit) within us accomplishes complete victory over the temptation. Faith in the fact of our death to sin and our vital look of faith to God constitutes the answer. Thus a new freedom never before experienced emerges. As John said, faith is the victory that overcomes the world. Not only in eternity are we delivered from the penalty and presence of sin through faith, but also by faith we are saved from sin's daily power. The battle is to stay on the ground of faith. Let it be clear, this does *not* produce sinless perfection. That happy estate waits for heaven. Recall what John said: "If we say that we have no sin, we are deceiving ourselves and the truth is not in us" (1 John 1:8). There are always new areas of the old life to conquer at the present state and level of our sanctification. But by faith in our identification with Christ, we can be conquerors in our Lord over what we do realize displeases him.

This is what it means to live a holy life. We walk in actual fellowship with the living Christ, daily being cleansed when we do err but exercising constant faith in our identification with Christ and looking to him for victory. He resides within us, and we are in him. He simply lives his life through us. That quality of life cannot be anything but powerful in Christian mission, for it is not our life as such. Christ manifests his life in us through the Holy Spirit. This leads to discussing the resource that is ours in the Spirit of God. To these principles the entire body of Christ should be committed.

The Power of the Holy Spirit

For our immediate concern, the work of the Holy Spirit should be seen in a twofold sense. First, God imparts the person and power of the Holy Spirit to the believer to make his or her life holy. We simply cannot live a holy life apart from the Holy Spirit. Second, the Holy Spirit demonstrates his power through the believer, thus making Christian service effective and fruitful. R. A. Torrey has correctly pointed out:

> The Holy Spirit is the person who imparts to the individual believer the power that belongs to God. This is the Holy Spirit's work in the believer, to take what belongs to God and make it ours. All the manifold power of God belongs to the children of God as their birthright in Christ. It becomes ours in actual and experimental possession through the Holy Spirit's work in us as individuals. To the extent that we understand and claim for ourselves the Holy Spirit's work, to that extent do we obtain for ourselves the fullness of power in Christian life and service that God has provided for us in Christ.[4]

All of this holds for the church collectively as well. Therefore, if one seeks to be effective in evangelizing our postmodern world, a proper relation to the Holy Spirit is vital. What then is the scriptural principle of our relationship to the Spirit of God that will spell power to live, serve, and evangelize successfully?

The New Testament makes it clear that all believers are indwelt by the Holy Spirit and sealed with his stamp. But the Scriptures also make it abundantly clear that God intends that all Christians be *filled with the Holy Spirit* (Eph. 5:18). A believer is not merely a possessor of the Spirit; he or she should strive for the infilling of the Spirit as well. Such a relationship with God's Spirit makes service powerful. This truth is forcefully brought out in the following passages of Scripture:

> And behold, I am sending forth the promise of my Father upon you; but you are to stay in the city until you are clothed with power from on high (Luke 24:49).

> But you shall receive power when the Holy Spirit has come upon you; and you shall be my witnesses in Jerusalem and in all Judea and Samaria and to the end of the earth (Acts 1:8 RSV).

> And they were all filled with the Holy Spirit and began to speak with other tongues, as the Spirit was giving them utterance (Acts 2:4).

And when they had prayed, the place where they had gathered together was shaken, and they were all filled with the Holy Spirit and began to speak the word of God with boldness (Acts 4:31).

And do not get drunk with wine, for that is debauchery; but be filled with the Spirit (Eph. 5:18 RSV).

Besides this weight of Scripture—and there are many other passages—effective men and women of God give testimony to the validity of the concept of the Spirit-filled life. For example, R. A. Torrey said, "I was led to seek the baptism [filling] with the Holy Spirit, because I became convinced from the study of the Acts of the Apostles that no one had a right to preach the gospel until he had." Charles G. Finney wrote, "I was powerfully converted on the morning of the 10th of October, 1821. In the evening of the same day I received overwhelming baptisms [fillings] of the Holy Ghost." A. T. Pierson said concerning his ministry after having been filled with the Spirit, "I have seen more conversions and accomplished more in eighteen months since I received that blessing than in the eighteen years previous."[5]

The issue therefore becomes, How do we receive the fullness of the Spirit and daily walk with his hand on us? First, we must confess and forsake all known sins. As much as we can know, we must be cleansed by the blood of Christ (1 John 1:9). This principle has been made amply clear. Then, there must be surrendering without reservation to Jesus Christ as Lord of life (Rom. 12:1–2). Finally, we should pray and simply trust God to do the work of the Spirit's filling (Luke 11:13). The very moment we confess all known sins (we all have unknown sins and can hardly confess these), surrender totally to Christ, and trust God to fill us with his blessed Spirit, he will surely meet our need and we will become a Spirit-filled Christian. It is that simple yet that profound.

Obviously, a definite relationship exists between being filled with the Spirit and walking daily with Christ. Unlike conversion, being filled with the Spirit is not a once-for-all experience. It surely does not bring one into a state of perfection, as some would teach. And there is no particular "gift of the Spirit" one must receive to experience the infilling. It may not even be an emotional experience, but being filled with the Spirit is something we are to experience each day we live. This is why Paul said in Ephesians 5:18 to continue to "be filled with the Spirit." So, as we walk moment by moment with Christ, daily coming to him as empty vessels to a full fountain to have our cup made full and running over with his Spirit, that strikes at the heart of it all. And if we fail to walk with Christ, we will probably fail to come to him for the divine touch of his Holy Spirit, thus becoming impotent in his service. To walk with

God, therefore, is to walk in Christ's power. When this becomes our perpetual experience, then the power of a holy life and the dynamic of the Holy Spirit will work to make our service effective. When the church receives God's touch of power, it will minister on a new level and with significant effect.

Furthermore, when we individually, and the church collectively, walk in the Holy Spirit's fullness, many promises of the Scriptures can be claimed:

- In the Holy Spirit we are set free from the law of sin and death (Rom. 8:2).
- In the Holy Spirit we are strengthened in the inward person (Eph. 3:16).
- In the Holy Spirit we find God's leading (Rom. 8:14).
- In the Holy Spirit we bear fruit (Gal. 5:22–23).
- In the Holy Spirit we are led into all truth (John 16:13).
- In the Holy Spirit we learn to pray effectively (Eph. 6:18).
- In the Holy Spirit we can communicate the truth to others (1 Cor. 2:15).
- In the Holy Spirit we can evangelize in power (Acts 2:3–41).

Thus we can conclude that apart from a vital relationship to the Spirit of God, one can hope for little magnetism for Christ and little power in his service. We simply cannot evangelize postmoderns or anyone else without the Spirit's working through us toward the unbelieving world. Also the Holy Spirit stands as the source of the evangelistic passion within believers.

The Power of a Holy Passion

David Brainerd, missionary to the American Indians, said, "I cared not where or how I lived or what hardships I went through so that I could but gain souls for Christ. While I was asleep I dreamed of these things, and when I awoke the first thing I thought of was this great work. All of my desire was for the conversion of the heathen and all my hope was in God." In a similar spirit, Thomas Chalmers prayed, "Recall the twenty-one years of my service; give me back its shipwreck, give me its standings in the face of death, give me it surrounded by fierce savages with spears and clubs, give it back to me with clubs knocking me down, give all this back to me, and I will be your missionary still."[6]

This depth of commitment God honors, and this kind of passion communicates to people. As John Wesley said, "Get on fire for God and people will come to watch you burn." This does not mean a shallow, vociferous approach in reaching people for Christ. That can be damaging to evangelistic outreach. God desires his witnesses to be loving, burdened, concerned, zealous seekers of the lost, spreading the message of salvation in love to the millions who desperately need to hear the truth. As we seek the Holy Spirit's strength, wisdom, and compassion, he will instill us with this attitude. One would hope that all Christians could become so committed to the evangelistic task that such a passion would grip the entire church. If this situation is ever to occur, it must first begin with fervent prayer.

The Power of Prayer

Prayer is a tremendous resource of power about which perhaps little need be said. In no sense is the theme secondary; on the contrary, it stands as vital. The reason for saying little here is that much fine material has already been produced on the subject; anything this author could contribute would be of little additional value. Let it be said simply that prayer is essential to spiritual power in life and service. We get what we claim by faith in prayer. Every great spiritual movement has been conceived, born, and matured through intercession. Whether we look at Jacob centuries ago, wrestling in prayer by the river Jabbok, or the recent revival that has come to many parts of the world, prayer has been the key that has opened the treasure house of God's power.

Probably one of our basic problems today is, "You do not have because you do not ask" (James 4:2). Would to God we could learn to pray sacrificially and lead the entire church into the ministry of prayer. In one of my early pastorates we had a weekly all-night chain of prayer. The manifestation of God's power in that little church was tremendous. God responds to his people's pleas. Renewal and effective evangelism wait on the power of prayer. It provides a vast resource for all Christians. Leaders in churches should develop ministries of prayer for God's people. Nothing is more important.

The Power of the Word of God

The "good seed" that falls in the ground and brings forth fruit is the Word of God: a *word of power*. The Lord said through Jeremiah, "Is not my word like fire, says the LORD, and like a hammer which breaks the rock in pieces?" (Jer. 23:29 RSV). Again space precludes an excursion into the interesting and relevant theological field of revelation and inspiration. What is important to realize here centers in the fact that the Christian has tremendous resources in the power of the Word of God. As Paul said, "I am not ashamed of the gospel; it is the power of God for salvation to every one who has faith" (Rom. 1:16 RSV).

The Bible itself has much to say about the power of the Word in the hands of the Holy Spirit.

- It serves as the instrument of the Spirit in conversion (James 1:18).
- It produces faith (Rom. 10:17).
- It is the means of cleansing (Eph. 5:25–26).
- It builds one up in Christ (Acts 20:32).
- It becomes a source of wisdom (Ps. 119:130).
- It gives the assurance of eternal life (1 John 5:13).

The Christian who desires to win others should realize the Scriptures are a most powerful weapon in spiritual warfare. Thus we can unashamedly and positively present the Good News in the full assurance that God will honor his Word of power and use it to speak to the hearts of the hearers. The proclaimer honors God when he or she honors the Scriptures by forthrightly in faith declaring their truth. This is why time was spent earlier discussing the basic kerygma, for that makes up the message God's Spirit uses to bring unbelievers to faith in Christ. One need not rely on human wisdom and ingenuity. As a matter of fact, if we do, we forsake the only real source of genuine power at our disposal. The Word of God *alone* is "the sword of the Spirit" (Eph. 6:17). It must be studied, cherished, and lived out by all who would walk with Christ in fellowship.

The Power of a Committed Life of Faith

In the final analysis, our discussion of the life of power could be correctly summed up by emphasizing the resource of total surrender in faith to Jesus Christ. God's work through the life of the Christian depends on that life being surrendered to God's will and purpose. Knowledge comes through commitment (John 7:17); prayer is dependent on a surrendered will (1 John 3:22); one's joy and winsome testimony finds its base in yieldedness to God's authority (John 15:10–11); and the Holy

Spirit empowers only those who present themselves unreservedly to God's purpose and plan (Acts 5:32).

Even secular psychologists stress the unifying influence and powerful impact of being committed to a great cause. The world, the postmodern world, longs to see those who are surrendered and committed to God and the evangelization of the world. It communicates powerfully to the contemporary existential mind-set. Moreover, the mission task that God lays on his people is such that only the resource and power of a deep commitment will see it accomplished. May God bring the entire church into that kind of surrender to himself and to the task of bringing Christ to all the world.

Conclusion

The question may have occurred, Why all this emphasis on the spiritual life of believers in a volume on how to evangelize the postmodern age? The answer is very simple: Our Lord said, "Apart from Me you can do nothing" (John 15:5). We have quoted this verse often, and it is true; without the Spirit of Christ working in and through believers individually and the church as a body, nothing of any lasting consequence ensues. We are laborers in kingdom ministry. And the kingdom of God matters most. We need a grasp of that principle and the nature of God's kingdom.

New Testament scholar George Beasley-Murray sees the kingdom as the divine *basileia*. It is God acting in judgment and salvation through the Son in a sovereign fashion. Through the Son the kingdom of God in Christ is established. Clearly, kingdom progress centers in God bringing people to his Son Jesus Christ. Granted, methods and knowledge of how to evangelize have their role, and they have constituted the bulk of this book. *But we need God* if we are to see his kingdom flourish. In the final analysis, our Lord is the great evangelist. We may be relatively uninstructed on how to reach our contemporary age, but if our Lord reigns supreme in our lives and church, we will be used to win postmoderns. Let us learn all we can to be effective witnesses and build an effective evangelistic church; but above all, let us walk with Christ. Therein lies power and therein lies the victory. That is the revival we need. May we pray, and lead others to pray, until the heavens are opened and *all* God's people are renewed to be true servants of our Lord. That is when this postmodern age will be met and won to Christ.

Questions and Issues for Study

1. Where does real power for the task lie?
2. What is that power?
3. How does one appropriate God's power?
4. How does one walk *daily* in the fullness of the Holy Spirit?
5. How does a person deal with his or her own sins as a Christian?
6. What role does Bible study play in daily walking in the Spirit?
7. What role does prayer play?
8. What role does abiding in Christ play?
9. What role does absolute commitment play?
10. How can we see real revival—personally, corporately, and even nationally? That alone is the final answer to reaching our post-modern era.

Epilogue

When the final tally is made, what stands most needed to reach our new age centers in a new, fresh "wind of the Spirit" in true revival. We need a genuine, spiritual awakening in our lives and churches. God has done it in the past: "God comes from Teman, and the Holy One from Mount Paran. His splendor covers the heavens, and the earth is full of His praise" (Hab. 3:3). Then multitudes are won to Jesus Christ as the church takes on new life in the Spirit. Above all, therefore, may we seek a mighty move of God on us to reach the postmodern age. It is this phenomenon we call a "spiritual awakening."

The Anatomy of a Spiritual Awakening

Charles Haddon Spurgeon tells of revival in his day:

The times of refreshing from the presence of the Lord have at last dawned upon our land. Everywhere there are signs of aroused activity and increased earnestness. A spirit of prayer is visiting our churches, and its paths are dropping fatness. The first breath of the rushing wind is already discerned, while on rising evangelists the tongues of fire have evidently descended.[1]

With these intriguing words, Spurgeon, the incomparable Victorian London preacher, described the refreshing spiritual awakening that engulfed his early ministry. What a time it must have been for the powerful pulpiteer! What was actually taking place?

The erupting spirit of revival, or spiritual awakening, as such movements are variously termed, had moved across the Atlantic to Great Britain from America, where it had already ignited and was spreading from coast to coast.[2] When it swept onto Britain's shores, it initially sparked Ireland. In 1858 the Presbyterian Church of Ireland had dispatched observers to the United States to investigate what was already being called the Prayer Revival. The spirit of renewal had virtually engulfed the entire American nation and was making news worldwide. The Irish observers returned home renewed and began to thrill others with what they had experienced. Soon Belfast, Dublin, Cork, and the entire countryside fell under the impact of the prayer movement. Ireland sank to its knees in intercession. The spirit of the Old Testament "solemn assembly" sounded forth, and the saints responded.

Wales also began to feel the breath of the Spirit, almost simultaneously with Ireland. Before long all of Wales caught fire with awakening power.

As the continuing news and challenging stories of the awakening spread throughout the British Isles, Scotland roused itself to the call of the Spirit. Prayer meetings sprang up in Glasgow and Edinburgh; soon all the cities and towns of the country responded. By 1859 the United Presbyterian Church reported that one-fourth of its members regularly attended prayer meetings for spiritual awakening.

Finally, England took notice and began to be warmed by the conflagration. In 1859 a united prayer meeting was launched in the Throne Room of the Cosby Hall, London. Attendance soon reached one hundred at the noon-hour service. By the end of the year, twenty-four daily and sixty weekly prayer meetings dotted the London area. In a matter of days, the number escalated to one hundred twenty; then the revival fire spread throughout the entire English countryside.

As 1860 was ushered in, the Fortune, Garrick, and Sadler Wells theaters of London opened their doors for Sunday evangelistic services. Even the very traditional Saint Paul's and Westminster cathedrals scheduled special revival services. The ministry of Charles H. Spurgeon opened into full bloom as the mammoth Metropolitan Tabernacle, Spurgeon's new church building, neared completion.

In Dorset people flocked to hang on every word of Evan Hopkins. He later became a key figure in the significant Keswick Conventions. Charles G. Finney, the great American revivalist, preached with tremendous effect in Bolton as the revival deepened over England. William and Catherine Booth of Salvation Army fame ministered with fresh power. Oxford and Cambridge universities commenced special meetings. Britain, it seemed, had prostrated itself before God in fervent prayer.

As could be expected, the awakening created its caustic critics. The secularists voiced their vindictives in chorus as they attempted to negate the positive impact of the movement. But historians now realize the Awakening left a legacy of blessing extending even to this day. During the revival, one million new members entered the ranks of the British churches. Not only that, the Salvation Army, the Children's Special Service Mission, the China Inland Mission, and a host of new institutions and benevolent movements were founded that still carry on. As Spurgeon put it:

> It were well . . . that the Divine life would break forth everywhere—in the parlor, the workshop, counting house, the market, and streets. We are far too ready to confine it to the channel of Sunday services and religious meetings; it deserves a broader floodway and we must have it if we are to see gladder times. It must burst out upon men who do not care for it, and invade chambers where it will be regarded as an intrusion; it must be seen by wayfaring men streaming down the places of traffic and concourse, *hindering the progress of sinful trades,* and surrounding all, whether they will or no. Would to God that religion were more vital and forceful among us, so as to create *a powerful public opinion* on behalf of truth, justice, and holiness . . . a life that would *purify the age.* It is much to be desired that the Christian church may yet have *more power and influence* all over the world for *righteousness . . . social reform, and moral progress* (italics mine).[3]

Such social and moral reforms are what a spiritual awakening can accomplish. And that is what Britain experienced in 1860. The refreshing revival season had arrived, and the Prayer Revival will always stand as a classic illustration of a true awakening. But the question still surfaces: What actually takes place, in principle and in final results, during revival times? Perhaps even more important: What produces a great awakening? The answers, of course, rest in the Scriptures. Therefore, we must turn to the Word of God, where we find the accounts of several fascinating revivals, which exemplify the principles of revival.

As we begin our biblical odyssey, seeking to travel the routes of revival, James Burns, in his classic work *Revivals: Their Laws and Leaders,* points

us in the right direction, instructing us to look for several biblical principles that normally cluster around a spiritual awakening. Of course,
the Bible itself must give us the full and final answer concerning the
nature of an awakening. Yet Burns's concepts can serve at least as a pre-
liminary signpost in our search for what all the Word of God reveals
concerning a true revival.[4]

A brief explanatory note is in keeping at this point concerning defi-
nitions and terminology. There are those who would draw a rather sharp,
definitive line between revival and spiritual awakening. They hold that
revival occurs among the people of God as they repent and spiritual vitality is restored. Then, they tell us, *spiritual awakening* sweeps the general community and many are converted. Of course, such a distinction
can be properly made; however, most works on the phenomenon use
the two terms interchangeably, as has been the practice throughout the
history of revival. Even the term *renewal* is at times used in the same
manner. Therefore, it seems wise in this study to take the more historic,
traditional stance and use the terms interchangeably. At the same time,
it certainly is the case that God first awakens his own saints and restores
and renews them before significant change occurs in the community.
The principles Burns sets forth will make that clear.

Burns's Principles of Spiritual Awakenings

The principle of the fullness of time. A revival awakens the church to
the reality that God controls his work and will give his people what they
need when and how they need it. God is recognized as sovereign. He
gives an awakening when his sovereign will pleases. A revival may come
quite suddenly and virtually unexpectedly by the church at large, but
God orders all the details. He is Lord of the harvest. In that context Burns
points out the other principles.

The principle of the emergence of the prophet. Revivals usually produce
great leaders. There have been exceptions, like the Prayer Revival of
1858–1860 that was largely led by laypeople. Still, normally one or more
significant leaders emerge in the movement. A classic example is George
Whitefield and John Wesley in the eighteenth-century revival in Britain.

The principle of progress in spiritual matters. A revival first and foremost generates new spiritual life as it surges through the church and
community. Evangelism, social action, a new awareness of spirituality,
and other manifestations always surface. Spirituality superseding materialism becomes paramount.

The principle of variety. Every revival is unique. No awakening manifests itself identically in detail with any other movement, even though
the same basic principles invariably arise. For example, the Prayer
Revival centered on prayer, while the eighteenth-century Awakening
revolved around great preaching. The Welsh Revival of 1904–1906 fea-
tured singing and testimony.

The principle of recoil. Revivals come to an end—sad but true! Martin Luther said that thirty years constitutes the outer limit of an awakening. Whether he was invariably right or not, the sun finally sets on
every revival.

The principle of theology. Theology changes during revival times, often
rather radically. The church returns to basic, conservative, evangelical
thought and to apostolic simplicity and doctrine.

The principle of consistency. Although revivals differ, certain vital spiritual elements always surface. Theologian J. I. Packer tells us about his
understanding of such movements.

Packer's Views

J. I. Packer, in his helpful book *Keep in Step with the Spirit,* points out
the following elements in a true awakening:

1. Revival is God revitalizing his church.
2. Revival is God turning his anger away from his church.
3. Revival is God stirring the hearts of his people.
4. Revival is God displaying the sovereignty of his grace.[5]

In essence, the church becomes revitalized, the community is touched
and changed, needs are met, lives experience renewal, longings are fulfilled, and great glory is ascribed to God. Can there be any doubt that
we need such a movement in our time?

Gerald R. McDermott put his finger right on the spot when he said:

> Evangelicals are frustrated because their attempts to transform American
> culture seem to have failed. After electing three presidents and sending
> hundreds of legislators to Washington, and despite influencing public pol-
> icy with blizzards of mail and armies of lobbyists, evangelicals cannot
> point to a transformed America. As Charles Colson recently wrote in *Chris-
> tianity Today,* "Belief in the Bible has declined and religious influence has
> been so thoroughly scrubbed from public life that any honest observer
> would have to regard this as a post-Christian culture. Gallup reports the

most bewildering paradox: religion up, morality down. . . . We've protected our enterprises but in the process lost the culture."[6]

God's people everywhere should cry to the Lord in the words of the psalmist: "Wilt thou not revive us again: that thy people may rejoice in thee?" (Ps. 85:6 KJV). Revival is actually our best hope. But will the awakening come? God *does* dramatically reveal himself in revival times, and he always discloses himself according to his essential attributes as *Father, Sovereign, hope, holy grace, power, love, and availability.* The very nature of God revealing himself demonstrates the need and essence of a true revival today. Simply put, we need to see and experience God afresh and anew.

Our Role

What is our role in assuring that revival occurs? Let's look at the often quoted 2 Chronicles 7:14. "If my people who are called by my name humble themselves, and pray and seek my face, and turn from their wicked ways, *then I will hear from heaven, and will forgive their sin and heal their land"* (RSV). This epitomizes all that can be said concerning God's disclosure of himself in spiritual awakening. The text not only unveils God for who he is, it explicitly shows his people how to respond in the light of his revealed nature. Actually the revelation of God is the beginning of renewal, for as God declares himself, a commensurate response is immediately elicited from believers. This is a basic, essential principle of renewal—God reveals himself and his people respond. Thus we cling to our Lord's promise: "If my people . . . will . . . then I *will*." And when God *does,* the world is reached. May we pray until God once again "rends the heavens" in true revival power. Prayer—*united* prayer—*brings* God. May God raise up a "praying remnant" in our churches to intercede until once again the Lord rends the heavens. This is the greatest need of the day. Why not begin in your church? May we lift up the challenge for a "prayer remnant" to give themselves to intercession until it truly happens that "God comes from Teman, the Holy One from Mount Paran" (Hab. 3:3) and a real spiritual awakening breaks out in the church.

A Final Word

No doubt it is true that few things in this book are new; they are simply time honored principles of church-centered kingdom service. But now is the hour to take them earnestly and seriously *and do them.* May God so revive us that we will rise to the challenge and witness great things for his glory.

Appendix A

Evangelism and People with Disabilities

W. Daniel Blair

With the signing of the Americans with Disabilities Act (ADA) in 1990 came a major shift in public policy toward people with disabilities. At stake with its passage is the legal right of all citizens of the United States, regardless of physical or mental "handicap," to full access to public services. Yet, while the ensuing decade of the nineties witnessed a long stride toward justice and equity for people with disabilities, it has become evident that political change is easier to achieve than *attitudinal* change. In other words, changing the law does not change human hearts.

Further, due to prevailing views of the separation between church and state, churches are not legally accountable to ADA regulations (although the bounds of this interpretation are increasingly being tested). The sad consequence is that churches often lag behind civic and social organizations in their outreach and ministry to people with disabilities. Thus the purpose of this paper is to remind the church of Jesus Christ— chosen by the Father, redeemed by the Son, and regenerated by the Holy Spirit—that we are bound by a higher law, namely, the law of love. Although as Christ-followers we are taught to respect and obey the law of the land, our ultimate moral and ethical allegiance is to divine justice and sovereign mercy. Hence we are called and commissioned by our Lord to set the standard for human compassion and righteousness so that the world may see and know the glory of God and the reality of his salvation.

Through personal involvement with a growing number of graduate theological students with special needs, I have become increasingly aware of a consistent lack of understanding in the church and in the seminary regarding people with disabilities. My concern also stems from shared personal experience with my wife of ten years, who was born profoundly deaf. Angela lived the first twenty-five years of her life in the heart of the Bible Belt before finally being presented with the basics of the gospel in her own native American Sign Language (ASL). The tragedy of her story is that she was in church constantly while growing up but was obviously overlooked.

Though this oversight was unintentional, it is far too common. Inaccessible facilities and inappropriate methodologies routinely prohibit people with disabilities and their families from attending church. Yet, if the remedy merely involved remodeling buildings and hiring interpreters, the discrepancy could easily (though not inexpensively) be eliminated. But the source of the problem is deeper than physical structures and special programs. The most imposing barrier is the common assumption that worship, Christian education, and outreach should be designed only for those considered normal, whatever that is. The flip side of this assumption is that all others must adjust and make the best of it or be left out. As we shall see in a moment, this attitude is the antithesis of the mind-set and ministry of Jesus.

Thus, to begin the arduous task of transforming attitudes, I would like to suggest four biblical premises for the deliberate, intentional inclusion of persons with disabilities in congregational life. As pointed out already, the inclusion of people with disabilities in the life of the church does not just happen. It must be intentional. As one fellow deaf minister frequently says to churches that are interested in starting a new deaf ministry: "You have to be *called* to this ministry, or it'll never happen!" The fact is, as the body of Christ, we are *all* called to this ministry!

Premise 1—A Biblical Basis

We must recognize the inclusive nature of the gospel and the personal ministry of Jesus. According to the New Testament, Jesus left no room for doubt about his attitude toward those whom society has tagged "disabled." From the beginning to the end of his public ministry, he gravitated to those with special needs, and he did so in the face of a culture that was extremely hostile toward virtually anyone considered abnormal, defective, or deformed. Persons living with disability or disease were commonly presumed to be objects of divine retribution and ceremonially unclean and were treated as social outcasts.

Yet, in stark relief to this cruel cultural backdrop, Jesus came onto the scene proclaiming freedom for the oppressed, justice to the marginalized, and redemption for the disenfranchised, promising a radical reversal of the cosmos in which the meek will inherit the earth, all of which was predicated on the uniquely divine act of atonement for sin.

In postmodern terms, we might say that Jesus came to bring equal access and opportunity to those in substandard living conditions, to give voice and identity to those other than the dominant social elite, and to alleviate the ravages of capitalistic imperialism and colonialist economic aggression. Jesus signaled the breaking in of the reign and realm of God—his kingdom, a spiritual realm—which he authenticates not by overt power and dominance, but by acts of mercy, or should I say justice, toward persons who are poor, blind, deaf, paralyzed, autistic, psychotic, neurotic, dysfunctional, and infected. The spiritual inclusion of social rejects is no tertiary "special interest topic" to Jesus; his solidarity with outcasts is such that he himself was crucified *"outside the camp"* (Heb. 13:11–14). Throughout the Gospels, especially in Matthew and Luke, Jesus relentlessly sought out people who had come to be stigmatized by society as disabled, handicapped, crippled, impaired, dumb, retarded, idiotic, mad, and even possessed (not to mention racially diverse and female). Then and now, Jesus' invitation, "Come to me, all you who are weary and burdened" (Matt. 11:28 NIV), constitutes the heart of the gospel. His call to salvation is truly universal, for behind each stereotypical label, Jesus addresses a human being endowed with the image of God.

Thus, considering the ministry of Jesus in particular and the Christian social ethic of agape in general, it seems ironic that Christian theology as a whole offers no systematic biblical treatment of disabilities. Among evangelicals, theological treatment of disabilities is virtually non-existent, owing at least in part to the false dichotomy of orthodox theology and orthodox Christian living, which fueled the controversy between fundamentalism and the "social gospel" early last century. Yet it is this kind of critique that conservative evangelicals like Carl F. H. Henry level against earlier fundamentalism, that it "did not present Christianity as an overarching world view but concentrated instead on only part of the message. They were too otherworldly, anti-intellectual, and unwilling to bring their faith to bear upon culture and social life."[1] Turning back a few pages further into our evangelical heritage, we find leaders such as George Whitefield, John Wesley, George Mueller, C. H. Spurgeon, and D. L. Moody, who indeed brought their faith to bear on society with such clarity as to literally transform their respective cultures. As illustrated by the lives and ministries of these torchbearers and by the supreme example of Jesus, evangelical truth and social ministry belong together.

Assuming that the gospel is not incidentally but directly connected to social context, what does the Bible say about people with disabilities? Is the Word of God silent on this issue? In fact it has much to say both implicitly and explicitly. For example, after Moses makes a seemingly convincing argument for exempting himself from God's call to ministry based on his inability (disability?) to speak eloquently, God begins to educate his servant regarding disabilities: "Who gave man his mouth? Who makes him deaf or mute? Who gives him sight or makes him blind? Is it not I, the Lord?" (Exod. 4:11 NIV). Again, from the earthly ministry of Jesus, we read: "As he went along, he saw a man blind from birth. His disciples asked him, 'Rabbi, who sinned, this man or his parents, that he was born blind?'

'Neither this man nor his parents sinned,' said Jesus, 'but this happened so that the work of God might be displayed in his life' " (John 9:1–3 NIV).

Resisting for now the urge to theologize (or preach) on these verses, let it suffice to say that the basis of the entire Christian theological system—*the Trinity*—was established on less explicit textual matter than this. How much easier it should be, prima facie, to cull out a reasonable doctrine of disabilities from explicit question-and-answer passages like the ones above, not to mention many more with strong implications for ministry and disabilities.[2]

Premise 2—A Matter of Practice

A critical question that has not been satisfactorily addressed by the church is this: Who is responsible for providing pastoral care for persons with disabilities? Although social conditions for people with disabilities of patriarchal and medieval (Western) societies were radically inferior to contemporary American standards, there was at least the assumption that *pastoral care is the responsibility of the pastor,* not of the psychologist, the therapist, or civil government. Further, before the invention of modern social sciences, the pastor's primary guide for pastoral care was the Bible. With the early church fathers, the Scholastics, the Reformers, and the Puritans, practical divinity and doctrinal divinity were afforded equal status as mutually supportive divisions of systematic theology. Classic pastoral theologies like St. Gregory the Great's *Pastoral Care* and Richard Baxter's *The Reformed Pastor*[3] anchor a solid historical tradition of a biblical approach to the care of souls. It's interesting that the intricate biblical analyses of human conditions by these pastors anticipated many of the problems and methods posed by modern psychological counselors by more than thirteen hundred years.

With the coming of the Enlightenment and the rise of critical theoretical approaches to the Bible also came the near demise of theologically reflective pastoral care literature. Analytical practical theology was reduced to how-to handbooks on ministry and was, in effect, no longer considered worthy of the status of science.

More recently, theologian Thomas Oden, who in his earlier years drank deeply from modern critical theory, has helped revive interest in classical pastoral care with works like *Care of Souls in the Classical Tradition* and *Pastoral Theology: Essentials of Ministry*.[4] Along with Oden, there seems to be a groundswell of acknowledgment that modernist dependence on psychological methods of pastoral ministry is inadequate for spiritual care and that the early church leaders offer time-tested, biblically based wisdom to every generation. In twenty-first-century America, a day when even the secular government upholds the ethical rights of individuals to fully participate in society, the church should be carrying the banner of inclusion and accessibility. In fact the people of God should transform the so-called specialized ministries focused on people with disabilities once again into common aspects of pastoral care instead of handing them over to "the professionals."

Obviously, for churches to embrace this ministry, the leaders must see the need and provide support. This is precisely why the issue of ministry and people with disabilities ought to be a standard component of theological education and training at both undergraduate and seminary levels, equipping Christian leaders at the front end of their careers instead of trying to remediate them midstream.

In her book *What to Expect in Seminary,* Virginia S. Cetuk depicts practical, contextual experience in ministry as the "hub of curriculum":

Rightly viewed, the field education program is the hub of the curriculum for the Master of Divinity student. Course work in the areas of biblical studies, church history, theology, ethics, religion and society, and pastoral theology are all potentially related to the practice of ministry. I use the word *potentially* because not all seminaries are as intentional about linking the classroom with students' practice of ministry as they could or should be.[5]

Evidently the Association of Theological Schools (ATS), the accrediting body for seminaries and theological schools of North America and Canada, agrees with Cetuk's assessment. Standard 2.5, under the general heading of "Institutional Integrity," states: "In all cases, schools shall seek to assist their students in gaining the particular knowledge, appreciation, and openness needed to live and practice ministry effectively in changing cultural and racially diverse settings."[6]

More specifically concerned with the master of divinity degree program, standard A.3.1.0 states:

It [the MDiv program] should educate students for a comprehensive range of pastoral responsibilities and skills by providing opportunities for the appropriation of theological disciplines, for deepening understanding of the life of the church, for ongoing intellectual and ministerial formation, and for exercising the arts of ministry.[7]

In other words, ATS expresses the consensus among theological educators and students that divinity curricula should be geared toward ministerial practice and that ministerial practice should be culturally and globally informed. In this spirit let me reemphasize that persons with disabilities help populate every culture group on the planet and that human disability is truly a global phenomenon. Thus the common response that ministry to persons with disabilities is a "specialized" skill, and therefore not incumbent on all ministerial students, is simply out of touch with reality. Marketing specialists who target the beautiful, healthy, and wealthy of the world might make such a claim, but anyone truly in touch with the ordinary people of any geographical, socioeconomic, or ethnolinguistic community is inevitably in touch with persons with disabilities. To get personal, each of us as individuals, unless taken by an untimely death, will sooner or later experience disability. And when (not if) that happens, I, for one, do not want to be placed on the shelf and listed as a "shut-in." It may be that God's grace will shine most brightly when I am least able to take credit for it, that is, when my flesh becomes "disabled."

Premise 3—An Issue of Integrity

Ministry to people with disabilities is not a one-way proposition. The able-bodied do not simply serve "the disabled." In fact many people with disabilities grow weary of being viewed and treated as invalids (try breaking that word down: in-valid or not valid). Like every other member of the body of Christ, people with disabilities who believe in Jesus are re-created in the image of Christ and thus infinitely validated as persons, and they are endowed with spiritual gifts and abilities intended for the edification of the entire body. Simply put, without these dear ones, the body is incomplete. Thus the full, unrestricted inclusion of people with disabilities is not merely a matter of mercy; it is more accurately a matter of integrity (wholeness) of the body of Christ.

Further, ministry to people with special needs is usually rewarded with special blessings, as eloquently attested by the late Henri J. M. Nouwen, widely acclaimed author, speaker, and theological intellect, whose calling ultimately led him to L'Arche Daybreak Community for people with mental disabilities. On settling into his new ministry, Nouwen remarks:

> Not being able to use any of the skills that had proved so practical in the past was a real source of anxiety. I was suddenly faced with my naked self, open for affirmations and rejections, hugs and punches, smiles and tears, all dependent simply on how I was perceived at the moment. In a way, it seemed as though I was starting my life all over again. Relationships, connections, reputations could no longer be counted on.
>
> This experience was and, in many ways, is still the most important of my life, because it forced me to rediscover my true identity. These broken, wounded, and completely unpretentious people forced me to let go of my relevant self—the self that can do things, show things, prove things, build things—and forced me to reclaim that unadorned self in which I am completely vulnerable, open to receive and give love regardless of any accomplishments.
>
> . . . It is here that the need for a new Christian leadership becomes clear. The leader of the future will be the one who dares to claim his irrelevance in the contemporary world as a divine vocation that allows him or her to enter into a deep solidarity with the anguish underlying all the glitter of success and to bring the light of Jesus there.[8]

Premise 4—An Evangelistic Priority

People with disabilities are one of the largest unreached "people groups" in the world. Termed by some as "the world's largest cultural minority," people with disabilities form a distinct corporate entity. Their numbers are estimated by the World Health Organization to range above 54 million in the United States (nearly one of every five persons) and 450 million worldwide. Yet these percentages are generally not reflected at the congregational level. If they were, a congregation of 200 would include nearly 40 people with disabilities. In other words, our gatherings and actions would function quite differently with the presence of assistance dogs, interpreters for the deaf, wheelchair cutouts in the pews, and ramps leading up to the pulpit!

Closer to home (Birmingham, Alabama), according to research extrapolated from the census data, "conservative estimates indicate 75,000 persons with disabilities within a thirty-mile radius of Birmingham alone."[9] To this I would add that of the estimated 35,000 deaf people in Alabama, no more than 1 percent are in church on any given Sunday.

After many years of consulting with churches about deaf ministry and special needs, there is no doubt in my mind that the people of God want to be inclusive. Granted, many still offer the classic response, "But we don't have anyone *like that* in our church." Evidently these respondents are genuinely unaware of the multitude of people "like that" living in and around their own parishes. Thus the burden of church leadership is to notch up congregational awareness of special needs in the same way we address the challenges of racial and ethnic diversity or the realities of our socioeconomic context. Christian leaders must make a conscientious decision to become inclusive instead of exclusive and to welcome and even celebrate diversity instead of requiring homogeneity. Once the issue of disability is brought to the fore, it is not surprising that people often begin to "come out," disclosing personal struggles with disabilities that they previously endured anonymously.

So there is really no question as to whether or not churches under the lordship of Christ want to minister to special needs. Of course they do. The question is *how?* I have often seen ministers' eyes seem to roll back in their head and ring up dollar signs when the subject of accessibility comes up. They mistakenly imagine that the only strategy for becoming accessible and inclusive is complete renovation, which would certainly prove cost prohibitive for the average church budget. It is a sad fact indeed that the local pub is often more accessible than the local church edifice, especially the older, historic cathedrals of stone, replete with elaborate staircases, massive doors, and tiny restroom facilities. In most cases the best answer to this challenge is a systematic, well-advised, one-step-at-a-time approach. Simply put, the fact that the church cannot do everything at once is no excuse for doing nothing. Again, a sensitive and willing attitude speaks more forcefully than physical structures and programs. And before leaving the topic of cost and effort, we must ask, Exactly what value do we assign to the leading of precious souls for whom Christ died into right relationship with God, otherwise known as evangelism?

In conclusion, there are hopeful signs of potential transformation on the horizon. The convergence of certain trends in both the church and theological education, such as increased attention to multicultural diversity, an emerging global perspective—which I understand to include the universe next door as well as across the ocean—and the aging of the Baby Boom generation seem to be creating fertile conditions for the birth of a wonderfully humane and godly movement among the body of Christ, which will teach us to celebrate the fullness of God's redemption in ways we never imagined. As Brett Webb-Mitchell reminds us in his treatment of the wedding feast parable (Luke 14:15–23), there will be "unexpected guests at God's banquet."[10]

Appendix B

A Diagnostic Church Survey

Perhaps as never before the church needs to take a fresh look at itself. Postmodernism is a real revolution, and to reach that mind-set is no easy task. The average church quite desperately needs to ask some hard questions as to whether it is geared to minister to the new generation. This need can perhaps motivate a local church to conduct a diagnostic survey of itself to see if it truly is alive to the young postmodern and able to get on their wavelength. The purpose of such a survey is to evaluate objectively the life of a local church so that its ministry and witness may become more effective to all generations.

Sincere Christians surely desire to see the life and ministry of their church enhanced, but before this happens, it may be essential to overhaul aspects of the present church program. Such an undertaking calls for objectivity, honesty, and not a little bravery. The suggestions that follow will provide in broad terms some guidelines for conducting such a survey. It seems clear that if we can come to understand just where we are in local church life, we can see more clearly where we need to go. Yet it seems few churches undertake such a complete look at their structures with the view to reaching their constituency for Christ.

We begin with the writing of a statement of purpose, or a mission statement. Books such as *The Purpose-Driven Church* by Rick Warren may be helpful in this process. Such a statement asks the question, What is the essential mission of the church, and how does it relate to our local church? A well-expressed mission statement should answer the questions:

1. How should this mission affect the aims and plans of our local church, and does it actually do so?
2. What should be, therefore, the aims of our local church?
3. Are the church members conscious of these aims?
4. Do these aims govern the development of the program?

After the mission statement has been formulated, the next task is to set out possible programs that will fulfill the purpose of the church. This cannot be done on a purely hypothetical basis. The programs must grow out of the mission statement to be sure, but they must be programs and structures that meet genuine needs of the people the church is attempting to reach. This demands a survey of the community.

Surveying the Community

The task of surveying the community requires much work and not a little insight as to what constitutes real needs that the church can meet, and should meet, in light of the mission statement. This will call for a number of exercises, as follows:

1. Prepare a map of the community, if possible, indicating by a colored line the area surrounding the church (show church location).
2. Prepare a description of the church's area of responsibility, for example, location, type of housing, age, industrial or residential, racial patterns, subcultural groups, institutions, problems related to its environment, and so on. Get good demographics. This will take much study and research. Of course, it may well be that some local churches will reach across the city. Still, getting good demographics is important regardless of the extent of the "church field."
3. Investigate, research, and evaluate the community needs that should be met by the church. It is important for the church to come alive to the world outside its own inner life. Jesus certainly

was. He was a friend of "publicans and sinners," and he reached them. So must we.

4. Evaluate the effectiveness of the church in meeting the needs of its immediate community. What can and should be done to meet these needs in light of all the new information gained? This requires a survey of the organizational life of the church.

Surveying the Organizational Life of the Church

Following are thirteen steps to take at this stage of structuring the new life of the church. It is something of a diagnostic survey of the present church life to discover areas where renewal may be needed if the church is to reach the new generation and thus meet subsequent needs on the basis of its mission statement. Again let it be said that honesty and objectivity are demanded.

1. Summarize briefly the history of the church and how it relates (if it does) to the present church and the pressing, contemporary needs of the postmodern world.
2. Evaluate and critique the church's constitution and/or bylaws.
3. Study the church property and buildings. What long- or short-term plans should be made by the church concerning its location and future building needs? How adequate are the present buildings to meet the needs of the community? What repairs or changes in building plans are vital for the present and future? Are you using the present building to the best advantage in accordance with the church's message and ministry? What other building resources are available?
4. Study the church services of worship. The church is going through a revolution in worship; and there are many other segments of present church life that demand scrutiny if we are to reach postmoderns. What is the program of church music like? Is this vital aspect of church life given proper interest and concern? Is the language that is used able to effectively communicate? What is being done to educate in worship? Are the services "alive"? What can be done? What should be kept? Do you understand the relation between worship and mission?
5. Describe the outreach of the church. What is actually being done? Is there an evangelistic emphasis that is alive, relevant, and actually reaching people? What is the record of successful outreach over the past ten years? Are the church organizations involved in

evangelism? How conscious are the church members of the need
and centrality of evangelism? How can you reach outsiders in this
postmodern era? What training is given members? How can you
interact more relevantly to different groups of people in the community? What are you doing in worldwide evangelization?

6. How are members received into the church? What does the
church do to integrate new members into the total church program? What plans are there for conserving and training new
members in the Christian life and church life? How adequate and
useful are the membership rolls? What action is taken concerning inactive members?

7. Take a serious look and evaluate all the church ministries. What
services are rendered to family life—before and after marriage?
What about the church's crisis ministry, i.e., in times of death,
serious illness, birth? What about the problems of broken families, delinquency, and crime that occur in the life of the church
and the community? To what extent is the whole church involved
in pastoral care?

8. Evaluate the overall effectiveness of the church's educational program. This should include the work of the Sunday school, youth
organizations, women's work, men's programs, and so on. These
questions must be asked: Is our church truly educating people in
the Christian faith? Is there any segment of the membership not
receiving teaching in the Scriptures? If so, what can be done? Are
the present church organizations in line with the mission? Is there
a leadership training program? Is the laity being taught and
equipped for ministry? Are all given an opportunity to exercise
their gifts of the Spirit?

9. Study the church plan for promoting and practicing Christian
stewardship. Describe and evaluate the plan of church finance.
What emphasis is placed on this important aspect of dedication?
Are the church resources geared to ministry, i.e., ministry that
meets real needs? Does the church spend its monies in such a way
as to encourage giving? What portion of the membership gives
regularly? How badly hindered is the life and ministry of the
church because of poor stewardship? What can and should be
done?

10. Evaluate church recreation, for old and young, and other specialized activities, e.g., drama, youth clubs, holiday clubs. What
sort of impact is the church making on the community?

11. Evaluate leadership participation. What proportion of church
members have some leadership role? In the light of the study of
the church organizations, how adequate is the church leadership?

How are leaders discovered? What training do they receive to do their job effectively?

12. Study the problem of coordination and correlation. Is the church well integrated? How do the organizations relate to one another and help one another? Is the leadership of the church's total program unified and harmonious? Are there "churches within the church"? Are there too many overlappings and duplications of activities and functions? Are members chained to nonproductive activity? Do all of the organizations live, minister, develop, function, and serve in the light of the mission of the church? Is too much power vested in a few? This calls for a study of the entire administrative facilities of the church. Is there adequate equipment, e.g., duplicators, computers, typewriters? Does the pastor do an unfair amount of this work? Could the load be shared by others? Are good records kept? Are they used and found helpful to a better church life? Study and evaluate the promotional and publicity plans of the church. Are the monies used wisely and effectively? Do these plans "grab" people in their interest; do they truly communicate?

13. What are the possibilities for media outreach—TV, radio, mailouts, and so on?

The purpose of such an extensive assessment of the total church life is to discover the church's relevancy to the postmodern world. This undertaking must be the work of several people. Perhaps a group of the key leaders in the church would be the logical ones to oversee the work. As already emphasized, it must be done with objectivity, honesty, bravery, and, above all, in the spirit of helpfulness, understanding, and love. Much discussion and prayer must go into the venture. The whole idea is for a local church to understand itself in the light of the official mission statement of the church and to attempt to bring itself and all of its activities in line with that mission on the basis of total lay involvement. Moreover, such a survey must not be just put on paper and laid to rest. It should form a backdrop for changing and updating the whole life of the church.

As stated, the similar diagnostic survey of the community is vital as well. It is absolutely essential that the church come alive to the needs of people it is attempting to reach. Every resource available to discover needs must be researched. The church must not entertain a ghetto mentality; it needs to get out of itself and become awake to the community. This principle cannot be stressed too strongly. Moreover, the mission statement must always be kept in mind as the research and evaluative work is undertaken. All this calls for a committee or group that will work hard with a sensitivity to people. The best minds and most spiritually committed in the church should be enlisted for this vital task, for out of their efforts will come the next major step, creating new, relevant programs and structures to reach postmodern society.

Developing Programs: The Purpose Statement Principle

The church survey previously outlined rests on the negative diagnostic side. This does not mean all the older programs are irrelevant and to be discarded. We do away with only what is actually ineffective. But the church must now build a great new program to the glory of God, one that is totally relevant. That will mean new programs in the light of the community survey and *in line with the purpose statement* of the church. That is the positive side each local church must undertake. But the rewards are well worth the extensive effort. We are to present God's Good News in an effective and relevant fashion that results in genuinely reaching the new era for Christ. Today's world is not looking for gimmicks or shallow promotional programs. The postmodern generation desires to see genuine commitment to meeting their true needs. To this they will respond.

These programming endeavors have been stressed in a few words, but surely their centrality to the entire outreach life of the church is self-evident. Every church must create its own ministry structures on the basis of its own findings and in the light of the mission statement. Again, much prayer, biblical research, and hard work are demanded.

Goals

A major move after the establishing of the church's programs to minister to the postmodern generation is to set goals to implement the new structures. The old cliché is right: If we do not have a goal, we will hit it every time. We need goals to motivate God's people and to provide strategies to implement the programs. Goals must have three characteristics:

- Goals must be challenging.
- Goals must be attainable.
- Goals must be measurable.

Adhering to these characteristics keeps the work on track.

No doubt much thought and planning will go into goal setting. It will consider financing, equipping leaders and workers, enlisting people, perhaps even building new buildings. But the effort of goal setting and the implementation of the work to reach those goals are essential to the task of reaching the community for Christ. It gives the church direction and motivation. God's people are then enlisted, trained, and used to implement the programs and ministries. Be sure to match people with a proper "ministry gift" to the specific needs and programs. Then comes evaluation of the entire process.

Evaluation

Such a program demands continual evaluation. If a new venture does not prove effective in reaching people in their needs, eliminate it and attempt another program that will be more successful. Continue to strengthen and improve the efforts that demonstrate a measure of effectiveness. Further, continual awareness of changing community needs is vital, and changing programs to meet changing and diverse needs is essential. As is evident, this sort of evaluation becomes a nonending process, but it is the only way to maintain a vital ministry.

Summary

There are basically four steps that church leaders must take to assure that the church's ministries are reaching our postmodern generation. They are:

1. Writing a mission statement.
2. Creating programs to fulfill the mission statement that are relevant to contemporary society.
3. Setting goals to accomplish the purpose of the programs.
4. Continually evaluating the entire enterprise.

Quite clearly, all this extensive work calls for diligence, commitment, and a deep passion to reach people for Christ. May our Lord breathe such spiritual health and power into his people that the mountainous task of reaching postmoderns will be a joy crowned with rich rewards.

Appendix C

How to Discover Your Gift

How can Christians know what gifts they possess? It should first be understood that there is no presumption in saying that you have a gift. No one earned his or her gift or worked for it, nor was it bestowed because of some special merit. Gifts are given to all solely by the grace of the Spirit in accordance with his will. The glory belongs to God who grants his gifts for his honor and praise. Now to the issue of discovering your gift.

Guiding principles for this process can be discovered from the Scriptures and experience. The following are some of the basic spiritual disciplines necessary for discovering your gift. I call them the Ten Commandments of Discovering Your Spiritual Gifts.

1. Be confident that you have one or more gifts. The Bible says you do.
2. Study the Scriptures; they have the answers to questions about gifts. Begin with Romans 12, 1 Corinthians 12–14, and Ephesians 4.

3. Ask: How has God used me in the past, *really* used me? That may give some clues.
4. Ask: What do spiritual people say about me? They may provide some clues. Others often understand us better than we do ourselves. Sharing can be most important.
5. Ask: What do I like to do? We like to do what we do well. When we exercise our gift, we should do it well.
6. Ask: What needs burden me? God may want me to do that service.
7. Ask: What challenges me; that is, what does the Holy Spirit inspire me to do?
8. Ask: What open doors are before me? What opportunities are present? God may be in them.
9. Rest in Jesus. Do something, keep moving, be disciplined. Be open to change.
10. Pray and trust in God's leadership.

Today there are pressing needs all about. People everywhere are desperately reaching out for help, every kind of help. If we are Christians and want to live a spiritually rewarding lifestyle, we have a solemn responsibility before God to step in and meet those needs. And God has graciously equipped us to do just that.

Notes

Chapter 1 Today's Emerging World

1. C. H. Dodd, *The Moffatt Commentary, The Johannine Epistles* (New York: Harper and Row, 1946), 29.

2. Ibid., 31.

3. Francis Schaeffer, *The God Who Is There* (London: Hodder and Stoughton, 1968), 15.

4. D. A. Carson, *The Gagging of God* (Grand Rapids: Zondervan, 1996), 41–42.

5. Stanley Grenz, *A Primer on Postmodernism* (Grand Rapids: Eerdmans, 1996), 6.

6. Ibid.

7. Bruce Ellis Benson, "The End of a Fantastic Dream: Testifying to the Truth in the 'Post' Condition," *Christian Scholars Review* 30, no. 2 (2000): 158.

8. William D. Watkins, *The New Absolutes* (Minneapolis: Bethany, 1996), contents.

9. Schaeffer, *The God Who Is There*, 14.

10. Quoted in Lewis A. Drummond, *Leading Your Church in Evangelism* (Nashville: Broadman, 1975), 14.

11. Craig Kenneth Miller, *Postmoderns* (Nashville: Discipleship Resources, n.d.), 15–16.

12. Harvey Cox, *The Secular City* (New York: Macmillan, 1965), 2.

13. Paul Musselman, "Evangelism and the Disinherited," in *Evangelism and Contemporary Issues,* ed. Gordon Pratt Baker (Nashville: Tidings Press, 1964), 100.

14. Georgia Harkness, "Evangelism and Secularism," in *Evangelism and Contemporary Issues,* 71.

Chapter 2   What Is Church-Centered Evangelism?

1. Quoted in Bryan Green, *The Practice of Evangelism* (New York: Charles Scribner, 1951), 16.

2. W. E. Sangster, *Let Me Commend* (Nashville: Abingdon Press, 1948), 14.

3. Quoted in Douglas Webster, *What Is Evangelism?* (London: The Highway Press, 1964), 105.

4. Robert Beach Cunningham, "Evangelism and the Challenge of the City," in *Evangelism and Contemporary Issues,* 94.

5. Faris Daniel Whitesell, *Basic New Testament Evangelism* (Grand Rapids: Zondervan, 1949), 133.

6. Leighton Ford, *The Christian Persuader* (New York: Harper and Row, 1966), 45.

7. Charles Haddon Spurgeon, inaugural address given at the Pastor's College Conference, April 1891.

8. *The Church for Others* (Geneva: World Council of Churches, 1968), 18–19.

9. C. E. Autrey, *Basic Evangelism* (Grand Rapids: Zondervan, 1954), 63.

10. Joseph Henry Thayer, *A Greek-English Lexicon of the New Testament* (New York: American Book Co., 1886), 536.

11. Ibid., 137.

12. William Barclay, *The Letters to the Galatians and Ephesians in the Daily Study Bible* (Philadelphia: Westminster Press, 1956), 171–74.

13. Ibid., 175.

14. Whitesell, *Basic New Testament Evangelism,* 144.

15. Autrey, *Basic Evangelism,* 66.

16. Spurgeon, inaugural address.

Chapter 3   Having an Answer to Postmodern Questions

1. Paul Tournier, *To Understand Each Other* (Atlanta: John Knox, 1976), 8.

2. Ibid., 49.

3. *Humanist Manifestos I and II* (Buffalo, N.Y.: Prometheus Books, 1973), 16–17.

4. Quoted in Tim LaHaye, *The Battle for the Mind* (Old Tappan, N.J.: Revell, 1980), 66.

5. Quoted in D. Elton Trueblood, *Philosophy of Religion* (Grand Rapids: Baker, 1977), 260–61.

6. Nigel Colder, *Einstein's Universe* (London: Penguin Books, 1979), 187.

7. Quoted in Paul R. Baxter and Lewis A. Drummond, *How to Respond to a Skeptic* (Chicago: Moody Press, 1986), 99.

8. Van A. Harvey, *A Handbook of Theological Terms* (New York: Macmillan, 1964), 66.

9. Trueblood, *Philosophy of Religion,* 260–61.

10. Ibid., 265.

11. Friedrich Nietzsche, *The Will to Power,* ed. and trans., Walter Kaufman and R. J. Hollingdale (New York: Random House, 1967), 506.

12. Ibid., 45.

13. Quoted in Baxter and Drummond, *How to Respond to a Skeptic,* 93.

14. Jean-Paul Sartre, *The Words* (New York: George Brazilliz, 1964), 102–3.

15. C. S. Lewis, *Surprised by Joy* (New York: Harcourt, Brace and World, 1955), 226.

16. Harold J. Brown, "What's the Connection Between Faith and Works?" *Christianity Today*, June 1980, 1232–35.

17. Quoted in Vernon C. Grounds, *Is God Dead?* (Grand Rapids: Zondervan, 1966), 55.

Chapter 4   Constructing a Christian Worldview for Postmoderns and Moderns Alike

1. Clark H. Pinnock, *Biblical Revelation* (Chicago: Moody Press, 1971), 11.

2. J. S. Stewart, *The Strong Name* (Edinburgh: T. & T. Clark, 1940), 69–89.

Chapter 5   The Proclamation of the Good News of God

1. C. H. Dodd, *The Apostolic Preaching and Its Development* (London: Hodder and Stoughton, 1936), 7.

2. Ibid., 8.

3. Ibid.

4. Ibid., 24.

5. C. H. Dodd, *The Moffatt Commentary, The Johannine Epistles* (New York: Harper and Row, 1946), 208.

6. Ibid., 25.

7. George S. Duncan, *The Moffatt Commentary, The Epistle to the Galatians* (London: Hodder and Stoughton, 1934), 50.

8. Michael Green, *Evangelism in the Early Church* (London: Hodder and Stoughton, 1970), 48.

9. Ibid., 60.

10. Ibid., 61.

11. Ibid., 115.

12. C. F. D. Moule, *The Birth of the New Testament* (New York: Harper and Row, 1962); Edward Schweizer in *Current Issues in New Testament Interpretation*, eds. William Klassen and Graydon F. Snyder (New York: Harper, 1962); R. C. Worley, *Preaching and Teaching in the Early Church* (Philadelphia: Westminster Press, 1967).

13. Green, *Evangelism in the Early Church*, 150–52.

14. Douglas Webster, *Yes to Mission* (London: S.C.M. Press, 1966), 18.

15. Ibid., 19.

16. James S. Stewart, *A Faith to Proclaim* (New York: Charles Scribner, 1953), 18.

17. Ibid., 50.

18. Ibid., 55.

19. Ibid., 82.

20. Ibid., 104.

21. Ibid., 110.

22. Ibid., 143.

23. Raymond Brown, address entitled *Preaching Today*, given at Surgeon's College, London, 1969.

24. John Ker, *Lectures on the History of Preaching* (London: Hodder and Stoughton), 33.

25. Andrew W. Blackwood, *The Preparation of Sermons* (New York: Abingdon-Cokesbury Press), 15.

26. Webster, *Yes to Mission*, 20.

27. Herbert H. Farmer, *The Servant of the Word* (London: Nesbit, 1941), 27–28.

28. Ibid., 56.

29. Donald G. Miller, *Fire in Thy Mouth* (New York: Abingdon Press, 1954), 34.

30. Quoted in Brown, *Preaching Today.*

31. Ibid.

32. Farmer, *The Servant of the Word,* 90.

33. John R. W. Stott, *The Preacher's Portrait* (London: Tyndale Press, 1961), 50.

34. George E. Sweazey, *Effective Evangelism: The Greatest Work in the World* (New York: Harper and Row, 1953), 159.

35. Edwin McNeely, *Evangelistic Music* (Fort Worth: Seminary Hill Press, 1959), 4–5.

36. Quoted in ibid., 3.

37. Andrew W. Blackwood, *Evangelism in the Home Church* (New York: Abingdon-Cokesbury Press, 1952), 129.

38. Quoted in Walter B. Knight, *Knight's Master Book of New Illustrations* (Grand Rapids: Eerdmans, 1956), 645.

Chapter 6   A Basic Theology of Evangelism

1. Autrey, *Basic Evangelism,* 13.

2. A. Skevington Wood, *Evangelism: Its Theology and Practice* (Grand Rapids: Zondervan, 1966), 1.

3. Quoted in Lewis A. Drummond, *Leading Your Church in Evangelism* (Nashville: Broadman & Holman Publishers, 1975), 36.

4. Autrey, *Basic Evangelism,* 16.

5. Culbert G. Rutenber, *The Reconciling Gospel* (Philadelphia: Judson Press, 1960), 41.

6. Ibid.

7. Ibid., 46.

8. Green, *Evangelism in the Early Church,* 53–54.

9. Leon Morris, *The Apostolic Preaching of the Cross* (London: Tyndale Press, 1955), 12.

10. Ibid., 54.

11. Quoted in ibid., 279.

12. Rutenber, *The Reconciling Gospel,* 48.

13. Ibid., 55.

14. *The Church for Others,* 75.

15. R. C. H. Lenski, *The Interpretation of the Acts of the Apostles* (Minneapolis: Augsburg, 1934), 355.

Chapter 7   Obstacles to Overcome

1. Gavin Reid, *The Gaggery of God* (London: Hodder and Stoughton, 1969), 20–21.

2. Ibid., 22.

3. Reuel L. Howe, *The Miracle of Dialogue* (Greenwich, Conn.: Seabury Press, 1963).

4. James Leo Garrett Jr., "Evangelism and Social Involvement," *Southwestern Journal of Theology* 2 (spring 1970): 60.

5. Richard Warren, *The Purpose Driven Church* (Grand Rapids: Zondervan, 1995).

Chapter 8   Equipping God's People for the Task

1. Green, *Evangelism in the Early Church,* 172–74.

2. George Goyder, *The People's Church* (London: Hodder and Stoughton, 1966), 9.

3. Quoted in John A. T. Robinson, *The Layman's Church* (London: Lutterworth Press, 1963), 10.

4. John R. W. Stott, *One People* (London: Falcon Books, 1969), 24.

5. Ibid., 47.

6. Quoted in ibid.

7. Roger L. Shinn, *The Educational Mission of Our Church* (Philadelphia: United Press, 1962), 66–67.

8. A. Leonard Griffith, *What Is a Christian?* (Nashville: Abingdon Press, 1961), 117–20.

9. Rodney Collins, paper presented at the Baptist World Alliance Conference on Teaching and Training, Tokyo, 1970.

10. Alvin J. Lindgren, *Foundations for Purposeful Church Administration* (Nashville: Abingdon Press, 1965), 60.

11. Ordway Tead, *The Art of Administration* (New York: McGraw Hill, 1951), 101.

12. Quoted in George Wilson Jr. (paper presented at the Baptist World Alliance Conference on Teaching and Training, Tokyo, 1970).

13. Marcus Dods, *The Expositor's Bible*: *I Corinthians* (London: Hodder and Stoughton, 1891), 278.

14. Alfred Plummer, *The International Critical Commentary: I Corinthians* (Edinburgh: T. & T. Clark), 264.

15. Alexander Rattray Hay, *The New Testament Order for Church and Missionary* (Welland, Ontario: New Testament Missionary Union, 1967), 177.

16. *An American Commentary*, vol. 5 (Philadelphia: The American Baptist Publication Society, 1887), 104.

17. R. C. H. Lenski, *The Interpretation of St. Paul's First and Second Epistles to the Corinthians* (Minneapolis: Augsburg, 1937), 496–97.

18. Hay, *New Testament Order*, 186.

19. Quoted in *The Interpreter's Bible*, vol. 10 (Nashville: Abingdon Press, 1953), 164.

20. Quoted in *The Expositor's Greek Testament*, vol. 2 (Grand Rapids: Eerdmans, 1951), 887.

21. William Barclay, *Letters to the Corinthians* (Philadelphia: Westminster Press, 1954), 120.

22. Lenski, *The Interpretation of St. Paul's First and Second Epistles*, 497 (italics mine).

23. Barclay, *Letters to the Corinthians*, 124.

24. Goyder, *The People's Church*, 35.

25. Quoted by John R. W. Stott, *Our Guilty Silence* (London: Hodder and Stoughton, 1967), 13.

Chapter 9   Spiritual Power for the Work

1. Reid, *The Gaggery of God*, 57.

2. James Stewart, *A Man in Christ* (New York: Harper & Row, 1935).

3. Steven Barabas, *So Great Salvation* (New York: Revell, 1952), 88–89.

4. R. A. Torrey, *How to Obtain Fullness of Power* (London: Lakeland, 1955), 31.

5. R. A. Torrey, Charles G. Finney, and A. T. Pierson, quoted in Lewis A. Drummond, *Leading Your Church in Evangelism* (Nashville: Broadman & Holman, 1975), 153–54.

6. Ibid., 155–56.

Epilogue

1. Eric W. Hayden, *Spurgeon on Revival* (Grand Rapids: Zondervan, 1962), 12.

2. The very first "wind of the Spirit" had an early, germinal beginning in Canada in 1857.

3. Hayden, *Spurgeon on Revival*, 57.

4. James Burns, *Revivals: Their Laws and Leaders* (Grand Rapids: Baker, 1960). Burns's principles are discussed in detail in the author's previous work on revival, *The Awakening That Must Come* (Nashville: Broadman, 1978).

5. J. I. Packer, *Keep in Step with the Spirit* (Grand Rapids: Revell, 1984), 225–58.

6. Gerald R. McDermott, *National and International Religion Report,* Standard 2.5 (Roanoke, Va.: Stephen M. Wike).

Appendix A   Evangelism and People with Disabilities

1. R. V. Pierard, "Evangelicalism," in *Evangelical Dictionary of Theology,* ed. Walter A. Elwell (Grand Rapids: Baker, 1984).

2. For a survey of biblical texts dealing with disabilities, see Dennis D. Shurter, "Jesus' Ministry with People with Disabilities: Scriptural Foundations for Churches' Inclusive Ministry," *Journal of Religion in Disability and Rehabilitation,* 1, no. 4 (1994), 33–54.

3. St. Gregory the Great, *Pastoral Care: Regula Pastoralis* (Westminster, Md.: The Newman Press, 1950). Richard Baxter, *The Reformed Pastor* (Richmond: John Knox Press, 1956).

4. Thomas C. Oden, *Care of Souls in the Classical Tradition* (Philadelphia: Fortress, 1984); *Pastoral Theology: Essentials of Ministry* (San Francisco: Harper and Row, 1983).

5. Virginia Samuel Cetuk, *What to Expect in Seminary: Theological Education as Spiritual Formation* (Nashville: Abingdon, 1998), 138.

6. Bulletin 43, part 1, pages 54 and 93, published in 1998 by The Association of Theological Schools in the United States and Canada, 101 Summit Park Drive, Pittsburgh, PA 15275.

7. Ibid.

8. Henri J. M. Nouwen, *In the Name of Jesus* (New York: Crossroad, 1989), 16, 22.

9. Unpublished materials by the Lakeshore Foundation, Religion and Disability Program, 300 Ridgeway Drive, Birmingham, AL 35209.

10. Brett Webb-Mitchell, *Unexpected Guests at God's Banquet: Welcoming People with Disabilities into the Church* (New York: Crossroad, 1994).

Lewis A. Drummond is Billy Graham Professor of Evangelism and Church Growth at Beeson Divinity School in Birmingham, Alabama. An evangelical senior statesman, Dr. Drummond is well known in evangelical education circles. He has served as director of the Billy Graham Center at the Southern Baptist Theological Seminary and as president of Southeastern Baptist Seminary. He is the author of more than twenty books.